GOD'S INFLUENCER

Antonia Salzano and Andrea Acutis

God's Influencer

Holy Advice from St. Carlo Acutis

Interview by Giorgio Maria Carbone, O.P.

Translated by Nicholas Reitzug

SOPHIA INSTITUTE PRESS
Manchester, New Hampshire

Sophia Institute Press
Box 5284, Manchester, NH 03108
1-800-888-9344
www.SophiaInstitute.com

Sophia Institute Press is a registered trademark of Sophia Institute.

paperback ISBN 979-8-88911-344-7

ebook ISBN 979-8-88911-345-4

Library of Congress Control Number: 2024952372

2nd printing

Contents

GOD'S INFLUENCER

Preface

I AM EXTREMELY THANKFUL to be writing the preface for a book that gives tremendous insights into such a remarkable individual.

I imagine that the canonization of Carlo Acutis will be on the same level of significance as the canonization of St. Thérèse of Lisieux. People ask the inevitable question concerning the life of any saint: What did this person do? In the case of St. Thérèse, the answer might not seem like much by worldly standards, but she was incredibly holy, and this is evidenced by the number of miracles and devotees all over the world. In canonizations, God has His agenda; it is God who confirms the canonization by granting the miraculous favors. In the case of the Little Flower, He wasn't just canonizing a saint but a spirituality, a little way of holiness that every person can follow. I believe this is also true for the life of Carlo Acutis.

In the canonization of Carlo Acutis, we have God putting His hand not just on a person but on a way of life.

God gives us the saints we need to lead us in the face of trials of a particular age; and the role of the saints in our lives is primarily twofold. First, they intercede for us. No doubt Carlo will be very relatable for young people to pour out their concerns for his intercession and for adults to pray to and ask his intercession on behalf of the young people in their lives. His intercessory power is already very evident from many stories, but what I am most excited about is the second aspect of his heavenly ministry: to be a role model and example for each of us, young and old.

Carlo shows us how to say *yes* to God and to His plan. He shows us that even in our modern world, we are all called to be saints. The greatest *yes* of our life is to say yes to the will of God so that we might allow Him to live and act in and through us. Carlo gives us a path to sanctity, and here in this book, we get a glimpse into the life of a saint through the firsthand account of the people who knew him best, his mother and father.

Four aspects of Carlo's holiness stand out to me as particularly relevant for each of us today:

1. Carlo had a great love for the Eucharist. Carlo did everything in his power to receive Jesus in Holy Communion as often as possible. His mother recounts how he went to Mass daily! He would arrive early to prepare well and stay after to spend time with Jesus. For Carlo, the Eucharist was the source and center of his life. If he can do it, we can do it.

2. Carlo had a great love for Our Lady. He accepted Mary as his mother and was committed to praying the Rosary daily. The Rosary allows us to enter into the life of Christ, to encounter Him in each mystery with Mary, our mother. For Carlo, Mother Mary was an integral part of his spiritual life. If he can do it, we can do it.

3. Carlo made it his life goal to do the will of God. Carlo carefully discerned what God desired of him. Yes, he enjoyed technology and played video games, but he also thought carefully about how to use technology in a way that was balanced and would glorify

God. For Carlo, discernment and consultation with the Lord was a constant. If he can do it, we can do it.

4. Finally, Carlo calls us all to evangelize our neighbor. For some, that happens through social media; for others, it is in one-on-one conversations. We have good news — indeed, the greatest news humanity has ever known! — that Jesus Christ is alive, He is present in the Eucharist, and He wants to be present in the heart of every human on the face of the earth. For Carlo, sharing his faith with the world was non-negotiable. If he can do it, we can do it.

St. Carlo Acutis, pray for us.
— Gabriel Castillo
The Feast of the Holy Family
December 29, 2024

#1

I begin by launching a provocative statement: "No one can come to me unless the Father who sent me draws him" (John 6:44). Doesn't it seem presumptuous to want to transmit the Faith, given that following Christ — the substance of our faith — is an initiative of the Heavenly Father?

IT IS OUR OPINION as well that the expression "transmitting the faith" needs considerable clarification.

Our primary task is less focusing on transmitting the Faith, but rather to live it with integrity.

We are first of all believers: disciples seeking to listen to the Master. We follow in the footsteps of Christ and above all we try to live in communion of life with Him. Therefore, if we are faithful to Christ, we will also be witnesses and will transmit the Faith almost spontaneously.

Jesus asked His disciples: "But who do you say that I am?" (Matt. 16:15). Our faith has its origin in the personal encounter with Jesus, from the fact that today and every day we respond personally to that same question that Jesus asked the Twelve. And even if we do not respond in the same words as Peter — "You are the Christ, the Son of the living God" (Matt. 16:16) — the decisive element is responding: *You, Jesus, are the Lord. You are God. I love you. I thank you.*

A very simple way of living out our faith in the concrete reality of each day is by praying together as a family, and thus we become "light of the world" (Matt. 5:14); in other words, the knowledge that

God gives us about Himself begins to illuminate our daily life. It also becomes "salt of the earth" to use the simple words of Matthew 5:13; that is, the knowledge that God gives us about Himself and about all creation starts to give flavor to every reality.

Being light and salt is also a metaphor of our task of parenting: cooperating with God, the Giver of life, we beget children. And cooperating with God, we raise them in a life of communion with Him. Our children do not belong to us; they are not ours; they are God's, who entrusts them to us to help them mature in the life of faith. And the first thing that children see, especially when they are little, is whether we are coherent with what we believe. And if the child notices some incoherences, he promptly points it out to his parents. Coherence in living one's faith is demanding, of course. But everything that is lasting and beautiful requires constant effort to overcome our weariness. Without tiring, without becoming discouraged, we entrust ourselves to God, certain that He is omnipotent and precedes us always with His grace.

In your question, you quoted John 6:44, "No one can come to me unless the Father who sent me draws him." Here we glimpse two aspects: the *initiative* of the Father, for it is the Father who calls us to faith, and the call to faith seen as an *attraction*.

Faith, like all the theological virtues, is a gift from God. Believing means knowing what God knows about Himself and about creation. It means participating in His knowledge from which love of self and of creation is born. Only God can grant faith. And this gift is offered to all people. The drama is that many refuse it, do not appreciate it, or do not even realize they have been given this gift.

God calls all to faith. And being called to faith means that God introduces our intelligence into His own way of seeing things. God created us as He did in order to call us to faith and to communion of life with Him. On our side, the call to faith means being attracted to, fascinated by, or as it were, struck by the merciful love of the Father, who reveals Himself in the life and the countenance of Christ.

For example, the apostle Paul openly confessed: "Christ Jesus has made me his own" (Phil. 3:12). Faith, both as adhesion of my intelligence to God who reveals Himself and as something lived out in actions, is always a response to the discovery of the love of Christ.

For many parents, transmitting faith seems like a mission impossible, a utopia.

Certainly, if we look at the world we live in, which seems to row against the gospel, we feel discouraged. Especially if we trust too much in ourselves and do not surrender ourselves to God, asking His help, the result will always be dissatisfying. We must not get discouraged by our limits and our falls; we must walk securely in the certainty that all things are possible in God. Let us ask Jesus for help. We know that transmitting faith is a superhuman task that requires supernatural means. God loves each one of us personally and knows what each of us needs. Let us draw from His treasures with both hands, receiving the very Author of grace who gives Himself to us in the Most Holy Eucharist.

The cosmos has its origins in the Eucharist, *primus* in intention but *ultimus* in execution, in the fullness of time. As Pope Francis says in the encyclical *Laudato si'*, "The Lord, in the culmination of the mystery of the Incarnation, chose to reach our intimate depths through a fragment of matter. He comes not from above, but from within; he comes that we might find him in this world of ours. In the Eucharist, fullness is already achieved."[1] From the very beginning, humanity has been gathered into one and directed toward the

---

[1]   Pope Francis, *Laudato si'*, May 24, 2015, n. 236, https://www.vatican.va/content/francesco/en/encyclicals/documents/papa-francesco_20150524_enciclica-laudato-si.html.

Eucharist. Sin interrupted, but did not destroy, the eucharistic plan of God. Throughout all the universe, order and harmony and all that exists have the Eucharist as their point of convergence. The dimensions of the Eucharist are cosmic, and all the extraordinary richness and variety of the universe cannot be comprehended without reference to the Eucharist. Every family that lives on the Eucharist and is nourished by it symbolically adopts Jesus and takes Him to live in its own home; the Eucharist becomes the highway to Heaven for that family.

The Eucharist reveals and perfects the meaning of life. Yes, it is a mystery of faith, but it is also the reason behind faith, the marvelous setting of faith, the synthesis of faith, hope, and love. It might seem strange, but the Eucharist does not have a specific place; if it did, it would always be something partial and limited. If the Eucharist were localized as normal physical realities are, it would occupy only a specific space, in a specific container. The Eucharist transcends the limits of place because it is Life, and for this reason its place is everywhere; it is all. In the whole of reality, the Eucharist finds room to deploy its fullness of being and vitality. I'm talking about the whole of reality as we behold it. Namely, in its documentable and discoverable extension, but likewise in its mysteriousness, which also has to be considered. The Eucharist exercises its reign — which is not dominance — in all this. Its natural habitat is Life.

But what about the material world? Which material works concern the Eucharist? What do we mean by material works? The entire complex of material structures, in particular the settings where the Eucharist has its regular and habitual dwelling in our midst, such as churches or chapels. In the collaboration of man and nature represented by such structures, we find an interesting combination of matter and form, almost a hint of the Aristotelian intuition. Jesus wanted it this way. But what is essential is the bread and the wine.

Since the beginning of creation, God's plan has been clear: the Eucharist was already in the mind of God. God was thinking of the Eucharist in the beginning of time, as He created the elements that were to constitute the wheat and the grapes. We can state that the cosmos begins with the Eucharist, *primus* in intention, *ultimus* in execution: the first in intention, and the last in execution. Perhaps I'm saying things that are too sublime for me. The stars that have hovered in the heavens for hundreds of millennia, the astral tempests that shake the universe, the black holes that arouse so much curiosity and make us catch our breath — everything indicates that the design and plan of the Lord pointed to the Eucharist.

This is the mystery hidden throughout the ages! The churches, tabernacles, and sacred vessels are like the hidden voice of the cosmos that makes itself heard and must be interpreted in this precise sense: these material constructions enshroud the most spiritual and mysterious realities we can imagine. They have the appearance of bricks, or marble, gold or silver, in simple or artistic productions; but in reality, they are imbued with the cosmos and evoke all the secrets of the universe, proclaiming that the works of God certainly aimed at this, to give us the Eucharist, which is the center of everything and should be so for everyone. With such a precious reality, everyone in the Church, from the pope to the least Christian, ought to leap for joy and enthusiasm and concentrate in the Eucharist all his or her energies of evangelization and draw from the Eucharist on all occasions. It should be our one obsession.

The Eucharist is the center of the ages. The hours of the day revolve around it, and time is baptized and confirmed thanks to it. What does this mean? The Christian who receives Holy Communion is called to decide in the full capacity of his mind and will to give his life a eucharistic, that is, consecrated, tonality. The Eucharist should become the reference point of his thinking, his speaking, and his actions, and also the yardstick of his relations with others. Only in this way will his existence undergo the radical U-turn needed to move toward our true destination, which is Heaven. There needs to be a unanimous agreement in families to place the Eucharist in the center. Having families oriented in this manner, even if they are few, will influence the parish community. What is manifested and occurring in nuclear families will then radiate in a special way outwards. If parishes wish to function and offer a spiritual center, they must succeed in uniting eucharistic families that will be the yeast that leavens the dough of parish life. In this way, parishes can become centers of attraction and impulse. Our Masses, homilies, confessions, and all manner of parish groups will breathe fresh air; community life will be strengthened as when St. Paul wrote in the Acts of the Apostles that they were all of one heart and one soul (cf. 4:32).

#2

"Faith comes from what is heard, and what is heard comes by the preaching of Christ. But I ask, have they not heard? Indeed they have; for 'Their voice has gone out to all the earth, and their words to the ends of the world'" (Rom. 10:17–18). Fides ex audito: Faith passes from person to person by means of listening to the Word of God. And the apostle Paul immediately refers to preaching. But before discussing preaching, I ask Antonia, what was the place of the Word of God in a typical day for Carlo?

AS A BOY, CARLO loved to read the *Illustrated Children's Bible*. As an adolescent, he meditated a passage every day; long or short, it didn't matter. Sometimes, for the sake of memorizing it, he would write it down on a piece of paper. In this way, it became his light, his compass during the day, his wellspring of continual meditation. Carlo knew what the Church teaches, that God speaks to us today through Tradition and through Scripture. I remember one of the marvelous passages of *Dei Verbum*, Vatican II's Constitution on Divine Revelation: "This sacred tradition, therefore, and Sacred Scripture of both the Old and New Testaments are like a mirror in which the pilgrim Church on earth looks at God, from whom she has received everything, until she is brought finally to see Him as He is, face to face."[2]

#3

Is creation also a way, perhaps the first way, by which God speaks and reveals something of Himself to man?

Of course. One speaks of cosmic revelation. This is what God offers to all generations, even before and independently of the historical biblical revelation. Cosmic revelation allows us to know that God exists and tells us something about His power and providence. It is the foundation for dialogue among world religions. But it does not make us come to discover the face of God, that is, Jesus Christ. And when we say that God speaks to us through creation it is the same as saying that God speaks to us through the events of daily life. Events are realities that occur within creation.

I love to compare faith with a lighthouse: just as the lighthouse illumines the darkest night and allows those at sea to reach their

---

[2] Vatican Council II, Dogmatic Constitution on Divine Revelation *Dei Verbum* (November 18, 1965), no. 7.

destination, so too does faith illuminate the darkest, most obscure, most difficult aspects of existence. Even death, like Carlo's death, which the world might judge premature, in the light of faith is revealed to be a grace. Without the lighthouse of faith, we stumble in the dark, falling in our obscurity, in senselessness and absurdity. With the lighthouse of faith, we begin to see a ray of light on the horizon, discovering that every reality, even the least, even the most tragic and painful, is part of God's plan of salvation, which always and only seeks our good. We discover that the difficulties, too, are nothing compared to what awaits us, the eternally beatific life. Carlo often said, "Like the caterpillar, in death we shall become butterflies." This is the perspective of the believer, looking toward the blessed life that God has promised and Jesus Christ merited for us.

#4

"I can do all things in him who strengthens me" (Phil. 4:13). Is faith capable of changing concrete existence?

I [ANTONIA] WAS BORN into a secular family that did not live the Faith. We were baptized, but we didn't go to church or pray together or talk about matters of faith. I lived in the center of Rome and went to Catholic schools just because it was convenient. I received First Communion simply because all my classmates were doing so. I went to two other Masses, one for my Confirmation and one for my wedding. That's it. I thought that sacraments were simply ritual symbols. Although I wasn't aware of it, I had a typically Protestant approach. I didn't think the sacraments were, as they are, the work that Jesus Christ, living and risen, carries out for my sanctification, my salvation, my happiness. They are signs and actions that produce divine grace in us.

I came to this latter realization thanks to the help of Carlo and Andrea, but above all, obviously, thanks to the mercy of God, which is never lacking for those who are sincere and strive to please Him.

#5

Holiness is not an aspiration but a "gift" that must be cultivated. Reconsidering the past with the clarity of hindsight, what signs can you now recognize as attributable to Carlo's holiness?

CARLO WAS BORN WITH several gifts that he was able to cultivate and mature. For him, generosity, obedience, and purity were connatural qualities, almost spontaneous I would say. I think every baptized person is created with great potential; each person is called to develop that potential through his or her own free will and own desires. Carlo was enlivened by the desire to please God: he did everything that might please God. When I meet young people today, I ask them, "Do you want to be saints?" The vast majority answer: "I'm not interested."

The problem is the lack of interest in the life of grace, in the life of communion of love with God. This is the result of the fact that, in the collective imagination, the saintly person is someone recognized as holy by the Church, in other words, canonized, because they received extraordinary phenomena like visions, apparitions, revelations, stigmata, bilocations, interior locutions, levitations, or healing powers. These are charisms, divine gifts given to a person independently of his merits, for the good of all believers. They do not in any way imply that the person receiving them is holy: for this reason, they are called graces *gratis datae*, as distinguished from graces *gratum faciens* (i.e., sanctifying grace, which is indispensable in our lives because it is what makes us holy).

Therefore, sanctity is something different. A person is holy because he or she lives habitually the theological virtues and the human virtues and desires what God desires. And so, indirectly, sanctity demands fighting against everything that hinders or slows the plan of God. The main obstacle is mortal sin. And the slowing factors are venial sins. Spiritual combat is an integral part of the Christian life. If I were not to fight, I would be left to the mercy of temptation, evil, and sin.

This aspect of struggle and combat seems to be forgotten by many today. Not only is there the disinterest that I mentioned above but also so much mediocrity, loss of enthusiasm, lack of ardor, and general submissiveness to "what everyone is doing." We must have the courage to call this spiritual attitude by its name: laziness, indolence, sloth. These are vices that we are called to combat with the virtue of fortitude, taking the initiative to act, loving the people we deal with, and loving the good that we do. The virtues, especially charity, benevolence, and mercy, transform our will and affections in a stable way, always orienting them to the good of the people we encounter. If, instead, we live in inertia and laziness, we subject ourselves to failure in loving.

John Paul II used a metaphor to describe sanctity: the saint is the masterpiece of God's grace. I love developing this metaphor in the following way: the saint collaborates with God in the construction of the masterpiece of his or her life and person. As with every building, sanctity requires a stage of demolition and one of construction. Demolition consists in fighting and forestalling one's vices, those voluntary attachments to evil, to sin—whether grave or venial. As distinct from demolition at a construction site, moral demolition lasts our whole life because the fight against some vices, like envy or pride, can go on for a long time. The constructive aspect is positive. Its cement is the constant and firm desire to be God's image and likeness. Because this is His design. And His bricks are the many virtues that Christian tradition teaches us but that we have been forgetting. I will recall just a few: magnanimity (nobility of spirit enabling one to do great things for the glory of God and for love of one's neighbor), generosity (gratuity in one's relationships), friendship (desiring and procuring the good of the person who is my friend), and fortitude (perseverance with firmness and constancy in doing good, overcoming every difficulty and danger).

#6

Does a saint always talk about holy things? Or does a saint talk about anything, but in a holy manner?

LOOKING AT CARLO, I'D say that a saint speaks about anything that's good, beautiful, or noble in a saintly manner. He would run from vulgar topics or demented things. Aside from that, Carlo interested himself in everything: in a city we were going to visit, in a political figure, in a video game, or in a computer program. And he always did so in a positive way and in light of the good of the people involved. When we were about to go to see his paternal grandparents, knowing that they enjoyed certain films, he set aside his personal tastes and went to get the video cassette of a film he knew would make them happy. Even in daily matters he sought to please God and make his neighbor happy. The examples abound of times he made friends with classmates who were disabled or victims of bullying.

#7

Parents obviously have an educational role and task. But a saint is guided by the Holy Spirit. Being in contact with a saint somehow impacts a person. What did Carlo teach you both?

IN CARLO WE SAW firsthand that holiness is a reality. We witnessed the Beatitudes of the Gospel come to fruition. From the very beginning, he bore witness to the spirit of poverty. Carlo was materially well off, but in his personal choices he was very frugal and sober. Boys of his age tended to compete to see who had more money, but Carlo broke with this social paradigm through his simple, humble way of acting. He was never haughty or snobbish but would take the initiative in doing humble tasks if he knew this could help someone. For example, at home in Milan he would help the lady who ironed clothes for us so that she could finish early and go home to spend time with her daughter.

#8

The greatest expression of the theological virtues of faith and hope is prayer addressed to God, to Jesus Christ. Antonia, do you remember anything that Carlo asked for in prayer?

TWO MEMORIES COME TO mind from the last summer we spent together. Both are from the end of August 2006. We were guests at his paternal grandparents' house in Santa Margherita Ligure.

The first was while returning home after Mass when Carlo, with simplicity and candor, told me he was asking Jesus what his vocation might be. And he asked me what I thought about him becoming a priest. I listened sympathetically, knowing how much he loved Jesus and the Church. And then he confided that he was asking in prayer for one of the most important things in life: to desire the way of life that God desires for us.

The second memory was when we were on a boat outing and we had gone as far as Porto Venere. Suddenly, from the surface of the water, a large school of dolphins appeared. As if they wanted to play with us, they approached the boat leaping and plunging constantly. Carlo's grandpa, who had frequented those waters his entire life, had never seen anything like this. Carlo was ecstatic, radiant. After a little while, Carlo very candidly told me that in the preceding days he had often prayed to Jesus, asking that before returning to Milan, He might grant him to see dolphins in the sea. They were his favorite animal. So, in his prayers, Carlo even asked for things we might consider trivial, just for the sake of the joy they would give.

The appearance of these dolphins was certainly a sign of the delicacy of the Lord toward Carlo. Since the time he was quite small, he had been the object of God's particular attention. Carlo's dialogue with Jesus was continuous. And Carlo told me that the Lord always fulfilled his prayers in some way. This was his secret to some extent: the fact that he lived in a relationship of constant intimacy with Jesus. He desired that everyone might be able to live this relationship like he did. He didn't consider it an exclusive privilege. And then, he would tell us with great simplicity to turn to God for all our needs: "He listens and responds. But we must believe; we must have faith that this dialogue is possible and real."

#9

A faith without cutting corners?

I REMEMBER AN EVENT from that last summer we spent in Santa Margherita Ligure. After dinner, while Carlo was finishing his summer vacation homework, we received a phone call. It was one of his female friends. Carlo, wanting to be discreet and not disturb me [Antonia] as I worked, stepped aside. But despite this, I could hear his words clearly. So, without wanting to, I overheard him. I had never eavesdropped on other people's conversations. And I'm not a nosy mother. But that evening, overhearing what he said was unavoidable. I was immediately struck by the way in which Carlo addressed his friend: he reprimanded her in a very paternal way but also with firmness and self-assurance. And then I was also struck by the content: as far as I could understand, the previous evening his friend had met a boy at a disco and had had intimate relations with him. Carlo was earnest about purity. He was not in the least a bigot. Rather, in the light of faith, he recognized that everyone has a special dignity to be respected, not consumed or devoured. He reminded his friend that "our body is a temple of the Holy Spirit" (1 Cor. 6:19) and that, through our Baptism and our life of faith, God "makes his home with us" (cf. John 14:23). For this reason, he told her not to jump ahead into what is reserved for marriage.

On other occasions as well, he spoke with his friends about this subject when they confided in him that they were getting ahead of themselves and wanting to engage in premarital intimacy. Carlo bore witness to purity, but not as an end in itself. Nor as mere asceticism or out of fear of something. His motivation was that love, even between a boy and a girl, must be lived as a gift of God and therefore in

His presence and according to His design of holiness. And only in this way can human love give an abundant harvest of happiness. If, on the other hand, we take a crush or a passing fancy for love and follow its lead, we will never reap the fruits of full and lasting joy. At times he seemed to be a priest talking. It almost made me smile when he told his female friend or other friends about the dignity of our body as the temple of the Holy Spirit, of the Most Holy Trinity. He said, "The Father has a throne in Heaven, and the Son too, who sits at His right hand, but the Holy Spirit has our hearts as His throne since they become temples of God. This is why we have to respect the sacred reality of our soul and our body, and not trivialize love, reducing it to a mere 'exchange of pleasure' aimed only at satisfying selfish desires and not at the true good."

When Carlo spoke about the passions and falling in love, he talked of how love is able to desire and do the greater good of the beloved, how it can renounce the longing to possess the other person, to subjugate the person to ourselves. He lived love in a detached way; it was not a lack of interest, but rather knowing that the other person is a child of God and therefore belongs to God. In personal relationships God is always present, for He is the Father of all.

I also remember hearing him scold several of his friends who boasted of looking at pornographic websites, of reading things he defined as "dangerous for the soul," or of practicing "auto-eroticism." He told these friends that in this way they became like the puppets in *Pinocchio*, the ones Mangiafuoco used in his shows and, after using them, threw them in the fire. With this image of the wooden puppets, he described the fate of people who, unable to resist temptations and letting themselves be overcome by vice, live like puppets: they no longer have self-control. Ultimately, they experience the total defeat symbolized by fire. To Carlo, staying far away from pornographic sites or from inappropriate materials was not about bigotry. It was the only way not to be contaminated, not to open the door to behaviors that leave a bitter taste in our mouths and do not make us happy. This is why he repeated to his friends: "Happiness is in loving others as God loves them and not in venting our selfish desires on others."

#10

Looking back over Carlo's life, do you think he had a method, a "gimmick" for transmitting his faith?

CERTAINLY THE EXHIBITIONS. PLANNING and putting together photo exhibitions was one of his passions. It was also one of his first thoughts when he came across something very beautiful. For example, at the start of September 2006, when we returned to Milan after our vacation, Carlo found a book dedicated to holy youth on his desk. He read it voraciously and then told us, "I would really like to do an exhibit dedicated to these figures."

He created several exhibits. One in particular, well received throughout the world, was dedicated to eucharistic miracles. From this exhibit, a book was published titled, *Eucharistic Miracles and the Christian Roots of Europe* (ESD, Bologna, now in its third edition), edited by Sergio Meloni. Carlo's name does not appear officially. We didn't want to expose him to publicity and preferred to use a sort of pseudonym, "St. Clement Institute." Carlo used the computer to create panels with photos, most of which he had taken. In the captions, he tried to present the substance of the miraculous event. Once the panels were put together and the exhibit was ready, he allowed the matter to run its course. And he was amazed at the success that always went well beyond his expectations. Requests poured in from around the world, without exaggerating. Just take a look at all the languages in which the captions were translated. Creating photo exhibits was Carlo's strategy for reaching many people and proclaiming to them the person of Jesus. He wanted to shed light on the beauty of the content of the Christian faith.

#11

But beyond this "gimmick," is there some aspect of Carlo's character and personality that predisposed him to teach the Faith with ease?

CERTAINLY THE FACT THAT he was always proactive in doing good. He stayed true to the original and unrepeatable plan that God from all eternity conceived for him, as He does for each of us. He coined the phrase, "Everyone is born original, but many die as photocopies." Of course, this might just be the indulgent regard of his parents. But the facts speak clearly. What comes to mind is the way he reacted when, after his first tests, he heard the diagnosis of the head physician of the De Marchi Clinic, "Carlo is afflicted, without a possible doubt, by type M3 leukemia pro myelocyte." Without dancing around the truth, he explained that it's a silent type of illness, without early symptoms, that provokes a very rapid proliferation of tumor cells. When the doctor left us by ourselves, Carlo was still serene; he broke into a large smile and told us, "The Lord has given me a wake-up call!" Even in this dramatic situation, Carlo showed his fundamental attitude: his ability to see the positive with serenity at all times. His smile illuminated our darkest hour. He said nothing that might reveal concern, anxiety, or anguish. He surrendered himself confidently into the arms of He who triumphed over death, entrusting himself to God, and so could smile in such a composed manner.

#12

I remember my phone call with you, Antonia, as if it were yesterday. You told me Carlo had died. I was amazed by your composure and the heroic serenity that transpired from your words in the midst of pain. How do you explain this?

IN HINDSIGHT, I HAVE to admit that Carlo's responses — such as "God has given me a wake-up call;" "I won't come out of this alive;" "I offer my suffering for the pope" — which seemed ironic at the time, in fact were the result of the way he looked at things, even realities that were dramatic and painful: he looked at them in the light of God's plan.

He lived with his gaze set upon God, in a communion of friendship with Him. He intensified this communion through fraternal charity, adoration, and participation at Mass. It was as if he were immersed in vital communion with God. The communion of life realized in sanctifying grace is the same as eternal communion. They are the same thing. There is no essential difference between the life of grace here and the life of glory there. It is always the same communion with God. It's just that here there are obstacles — for example, we run the risk of committing sin; our will fluctuates; it is not always stable in loving and believing — whereas there, communion is full, total, *overflowing*. Jesus says this clearly when speaking about the Last Judgment: "Be merciful, even as your Father is merciful. Judge not, and you will not be judged; condemn not, and you will not be condemned; forgive, and you will be forgiven; give, and it will be given to you; *good measure, pressed down, shaken together, running over*, will be put into your lap. For the measure you give will be the measure you get back" (Luke 6:36–38).

From this perspective, we can understand today how Carlo helped us to face death prepared. Of course we suffered, but we were not sad. We were neither desperate nor anguished but, as you correctly recalled, serene. We had interiorized the assurances of faith: we can pass though death, even when precocious and dramatic, together with Jesus, who from His death has gained for all a life of glory. When inquisitive friends questioned Carlo about the future, he would respond, "We have no stable city here below, but we seek the one to come. We have been raised to the supernatural plane, redeemed and saved. We are destined to eternity with God, our 'co-eternity.' Death is not the end of everything. It is not the end. It is not our ruin. It is not a fatal conclusion. It is the passage into co-eternity. If we see ourselves as sojourners in this world, if we keep in mind that our lives here are only temporary, if we aspire to the things above, if we wager everything on what is Beyond, if we base our existence on the Afterlife, then everything falls into place; everything finds balance; everything is rightly directed; everything takes on hope. If we think about tomorrow as a coming moment to be prepared, then one of the most important virtues in spirituality comes into play: hope. We're not talking here about hope in the sense of poetic flights or sentimental flair, nor as an evasion that lets us remain uninvolved, but true hope: the second theological virtue infused like a seed at our Baptism."

Then he invited his friends to pay attention to some of their habitual ways of speaking: "We often use the words *here, there, above, below*. This way of thinking and speaking relativizes everything. Being immersed in the here and now, we place everything in relation to time and space, which enslave us and condition us. If we disconnect ourselves from these chains, if we habituate ourselves to what is above and enter into intimacy with what lies Beyond, if we consider life a trampoline for Eternity, then death becomes a passage, a doorway, a means. It loses its drama. It loses its fatality. It loses its definitiveness. We exorcise death. We spiritualize death. We sanctify death. This is the secret. Then we stop thinking and talking and measuring in terms of its absoluteness—as a no-return, as total destruction—and instead we see death in the light, the warmth, and the victory of the Risen Christ."

#13

Antonia, you've often mentioned openly that, in one of the most difficult moments — when you saw Carlo's body in the coffin — in your memory the voice of Carlo emerged.

YES, HIS WORDS CAME clearly to mind: "Mamma, even if all our dreams should fall apart, we must never allow cynicism to get the upper hand and harden our hearts. From every disappointment a new dream will arise." He expressed his profound optimism in this. I have learned from Carlo's death that, although everything might suggest otherwise, we must never stop dreaming passionately and being optimistic. The future is not in our hands, fortunately! But neither is it in the hands of capricious "fate." The future is in God. Or rather, God is our future. God, Jesus dead and risen, is the goal, the finish line of our earthly existence. This consideration derived from our faith fills us with hope: death has been definitively defeated because it is nothing other than the door to Eternity.

This awareness does not lead to disengagement in the life of here and now, as Carlo said; it is not a flight toward paradise in complete disinterest in the present. The opposite is true. Given the indisputable fact that God is my future, I am committed to the present knowing that it is the only path into the future. I must learn to live passionately now in the reality that surrounds me, orienting everything toward God. In this way, I broaden my horizons and take flight into dimensions I could otherwise never reach. The real, the present moment, if it is illuminated by faith, allows us to rend the veils and transcend our small world, made up of appearances and contradictions, and open ourselves to the Infinite.

Carlo's words are most appropriate concerning these matters: "Our existence on this planet Earth has meaning. It has meaning if we understand it as a direct, personal path toward the Savior. So all our focus—mine and yours—should be to hasten this encounter, to bring it about and make it more concrete."

#14

On the theme of faith and friendship, what about prayer for friends?

As a jovial and lively youth, Carlo had many friends. He spent a lot of time with them. He prayed for them and united little sacrifices, *fioretti*, to his prayers for their authentic good. Friendship was a very important human virtue for him. In *The Little Prince*, which was a decisive book for his life, he read about the fox who said, "It is the time you have wasted for your rose that makes your rose so important."[3]

---

[3]   Antoine de Saint-Exupéry, *The Little Prince*, tr. Katherine Woods (London: Pan Books, 1974), 70.

Carlo understood that the time dedicated to a friend made that person special, unique, important. And that time must have charity at its center, namely the love that God Himself has for each of us. This time — however brief or long — becomes quality time.

So, it was quite normal for him, even when we were not in Milan, to make his presence felt, to show interest in his friends using the telephone or the Internet. He listened to them and shared his interests with them.

The vast network of friendships he created manifested itself fully on the occasion of his funeral. Our parish, Santa Maria Segreta in Milan, was packed with people we had never seen before. It was a mixed crowd of people of different ages, geographical origins, and professions. Everyone was crying. And at the same time, you could feel something positive, beautiful, as if it were not a funeral taking place, but rather a party. In fact, for Carlo it was a passage from this life to the blessed life. Our joy also arose from the gratitude this crowd of people expressed for Carlo. You can't imagine what an extraordinary thing this was.

Take, for instance, Neel, a man from Sri Lanka, who was the sacristan in our parish. Neel was amazed by Carlo's behavior, very different from that of his peers, and recognized that Carlo was not only respectful but also amiable and a friend to all. For example, Neel recalled how Carlo never yelled and was always courteous, and above all how Carlo always greeted him with a cheerful smile. After Carlo's death, Neel brought us a poem he had dedicated to him, written when he was still alive. We thought Carlo had been his best friend. In reality, we were amazed by the fact that Neel had never spoken directly with Carlo. Our son simply said hello and smiled when he crossed paths with him.

A simple hello, a cheerful smile, were like golden arrows that had struck the heart of Neel.

By gestures within everyone's reach, Carlo gives us a masterful lesson: every instant can be different if we live it with the right intensity. Attention to the other, even in little gestures, is never insignificant. A smile, a cordial greeting, thoughtfulness in our words—these always leave a mark. Mother Teresa of Calcutta often said, "We'll never know how much good a simple smile can do and that there is no better moment than now for being happy."

On his way home from school, he would stop to greet the doormen in the buildings along our street, most of whom are not Europeans. Carlo became friends with them all; any form of discrimination or snobbery was utterly foreign to him. In him, walls of indifference, hatred, or suspicion fell to pieces. He greeted everyone cheerfully; he chatted with everyone; he saw in everyone the image of Jesus Christ because every person is created in the image of Christ, the perfect image of the Father.

#15

Carlo would say, "A step in faith is a step closer to being and a step away from having." Do you remember the meaning Carlo gave to this phrase?

I THINK I CAN trace the meaning of Carlo's words here to an event that happened one night in August of 2006. We had gone out to eat in Portofino. As we were leaving the restaurant, Carlo stepped aside with a thoughtful and melancholy air about him. Every now and then he would do this. I didn't say anything to him. I didn't want to be intrusive. Perhaps he would tell me something later. And so he did. Before going to bed, he told me that as he left the restaurant, the words of Jesus resounded in his soul: "I thirst" (John 19:28). Jesus pronounced them during His Passion just before expiring. According to Carlo, the Lord wanted to make him understand His will through these words. As if to say: *My divine will does not care for the riches and luxury that surround you in Portofino; they are things that do not count. But look to the salvation of individual people that are here in Portofino; these do indeed count.*

Possessing does not give stable happiness. The way of being that comes from faith opens up for us a happiness that lasts forever. It is not wealth that gives happiness. Our main care should be the salvation of souls — our own and those of the people we encounter. After all, Jesus said the same: "For what will it profit a man, if he gains the whole world and forfeits his life?" (Matt. 16:26). Carlo would say, "If God possesses our heart, we will possess Infinity. Whoever trusts only in material goods and not in the Lord is living life backward. He is like a driver who, instead of going swiftly straight toward his destination, travels on the wrong side of the road and in the wrong direction, constantly risking a head-on collision."

#16

But if, during the first years of Carlo's life, you, Antonia, had an immature faith, and you, Andrea, did not attend church, who transmitted the rudiments of the Faith to Carlo?

THE PRESENCE IN OUR house of Beata, a Polish girl, was decisive. She was his nanny from 1992 until 1996. It was Beata who introduced him to the life of faith and its simplest practices, such as reciting the Rosary and praying for the faithful departed. When she first entered our home, her bag was full of prayer cards of the Madonna of Czestochowa. It was Beata who helped him to grasp the continuity between everyday life and the spiritual life, in communion with Jesus. Beata also helped me [Antonia] to live the sudden death of my father with a Christian spirit. When she was still in Poland, she lived through the final years of the Communist regime, which made life very difficult for believers. She was quite used to overcoming difficulties with fortitude. Beata often confided to us her impressions of our child. She said he was very precocious, that he asked the questions of a wise adult, that he had a great desire for a spiritual life. Carlo often wanted her to tell him stories about Jesus. When they went to Mass together, Carlo showed her his displeasure at not being able to receive Communion.

The beautiful relationship that developed between them did not inhibit Beata from observing that, in her opinion, Carlo was too subservient. Of course, he was very vivacious, sociable, and playful, as would be expected of a child his age. He was also very obedient to us, his parents, never giving us problems and always docile to our requests. But Beata pointed out how he *never* rebelled, not even when his classmates played tricks on him or mistreated him. Beata wanted Carlo to react and not allow himself to be made fun of. Carlo, for his part, responded with disarming simplicity, "Jesus would not be happy if I reacted with violence."

We can remember quite clearly something that happened when Carlo was about four years old. Beata and my mother had entered a supermarket, while Carlo and I remained outside. A girl with red, curly hair approached Carlo and started hitting him with a blue balloon. Maybe she just wanted to play with him. Or maybe she did it on purpose. But Carlo was impassible. Then the girl started making faces at him and even blowing raspberries. But Carlo still did not react. He only looked at her with sweetness and smiled at her. At this point, the little girl was thrown off by Carlo's smile and smiled too.

Carlo was giving proof of his strong character. He knew what he wanted: he was organizing his life around friendship with Jesus and taking Him as his model. His inspiration was Jesus, whom he knew dwelt in him by sanctifying grace.

Beata surely had an important role in educating him in the life of faith and its simple gestures. But looking back, we have to admit that if Carlo was docile and obedient to us, his parents, he was even more docile and attentive in corresponding with intelligence and promptness to divine grace, to the movements of the Holy Spirit, and to the imitation of Jesus. In his early years, we did not understand the importance of praying as a family, participating in Mass, or corresponding to friendship with God always and in every moment. Therefore, we were in no way capable of guiding him. We did not get in his way, however, and insofar as we could understand him, we encouraged him. We also understood that he wanted us to begin this journey toward God. So it was he — by his behavior, his desires, his curious and at times even impertinent questions — who dragged us into discovering the heart of Christian faith: to follow Christ, living in communion of life with Him and acting always in His presence.

#17

So, Carlo drew you into the Faith. How did that happen, concretely?

HIS GRANDPARENTS GAVE HIM the *Illustrated Bible* as a gift, and Carlo read it with passion. He also devoured the lives of the saints, the ones written for children or adolescents. Beata got him into the habit of entering church to greet Jesus present in the tabernacle. Thus, when Beata returned to Poland and we were the ones who went out with him, Carlo started asking us to go into church because he wanted to greet Jesus. He would go in, approach the altar and kneel either at the altar rail or in the first pew, and then prayed in silence. At first, we admired him. Later, we started to imitate him and pray in silence and then out loud with him.

It was his questions, at times insistent, that drew us to live our faith with greater seriousness and awareness. In those years, I [Antonia] was completely illiterate in matters of faith. For example, I didn't even know the difference between the Bible and the Gospel. Speaking for myself (Andrea has taken a different route), I was incapable of answering many of Carlo's questions. For this reason, I started studying the *Catechism of the Catholic Church* promulgated by John Paul II, published in 1992.

Then, we understood that the seriousness of life required us to seek the guidance of a wise person, a holy confessor. A friend suggested we speak with a priest in Bologna, Fr. Ilio Carrai. And so, in springtime 1995 we met him for the first time. He became our guide until his death on March 14, 2010. When he saw us for the first time, he amazed us by saying that he had been waiting for us for years and that we had an important mission to accomplish. He certainly had charismatic gifts: when we confessed to him, he already knew things from our past. And regarding the future, he spoke about Carlo: "God has chosen him for a special task." Then he narrated the details of what would happen in the years to come.

Fr. Ilio Carrai counseled us to deepen our understanding of the content of our Faith by reading Sacred Scripture and the *Catechism*. He suggested that I study theology at a Catholic university, which I did in Milan, attending classes and passing exams. Given Carlo's lively interest in the saints, Father suggested we buy documentaries and films on the lives of some of the saints and on the apparitions of the Blessed Virgin Mary. And you can't imagine how delighted Carlo was.

Carlo's faith was as simple as it was attractive. We noticed this as he lit candles and then prayed in silence before the Crucifix in church, or at home when he blew kisses to the statue of the Child Jesus or the Crucifix hanging on the wall in his room. Joy exuded from him when we gave him a medal of the scapular of Our Lady of Mt. Carmel. It was a precious gift from one of our great-grandmothers. On one side was the image of the Sacred Heart of Jesus, on the other [the Immaculate Heart] of Our Lady. He always wore this medal. And as he put it on, he said, "This way I'll have Jesus and Mary always next to my heart."

#18

Did Carlo have a plan for his life?

CARLO WAS MATURE AS a child and mature as an adolescent. He didn't waste time, but rather used it in the best way possible. Carlo always repeated that time and life are a gift that God gives us to be used well. And to him, "well" meant growing in charity toward God and one's neighbor. And the better this growth is, the greater our eternal beatitude will be in the life to come. He also wrote:

> Every minute that goes by is a minute fewer we have to grow
> in holiness, and time should not be wasted on things that are
> not pleasing to God, but we have to make time our ally.

This was his invitation to make the most of time, to render it quality time by living the virtues.

Always having Jesus as his point of reference, Carlo would say that Jesus showed us how best to use our time by becoming incarnate. Through the Incarnation of the eternal Word of God, Eternity manifested Himself openly in time and is now already giving each of us the possibility of living in communion with Him. This is the sense of *Kairos*, the time that is the today of salvation, that gives us access to God, to the Trinity, to Eternity. He knew that this today, beyond being a precious gift of God, is also a trial. A trial to not fall away from or reject the will of God for us, but rather to grow in harmony with it, to grow in the love of charity. For this reason, he was convinced that the sacraments are the greatest resource that God gives us on a regular basis to orient all our time toward Him. He once said to us, "Our destination must be Infinity, not finiteness."

He wrote a plan for his life a few days after receiving his First Communion: "To be always united to Jesus, this is the plan for my life." His fundamental priority was to eliminate everything that in any way might distance him from God; it was his commitment to personal conversion. "Conversion," as Carlo wrote, "is nothing other than shifting one's gaze from low to high. A simple movement of the eyes is enough." And when he said this, he did so with a tone and manner somewhere between serious and playful; with his sympathetic, buoyant manner and with metaphors, he knew how to communicate a great Christian truth.

"Conversion is halting our downward plunge and beginning to climb upward. The lower we have plunged, the more difficult and strenuous the climb upward will be. What is important is to change directions. Step by step, day after day, moving forward without ever stopping. The higher we climb, the more we shall see things from the right perspective, in their entirety and totality. The higher we climb, the more we enter the atmosphere that surrounds co-eternity. We shall then breathe the air of Infinity."

Wanting his conversion to be sincere and constant, he decided to go to Confession frequently, at least once every week. He almost always confessed to a priest who worked in our parish in Milan. This priest testified to us that Carlo was a very pure boy, desiring to improve in all things, both in love toward God and in love toward his neighbor, beginning with his parents. He desired to grow in friendship with his peers, classmates, and teachers. He wanted to dedicate himself earnestly to deepening his knowledge of school subjects and computer science, as well as subjects connected to faith. And at the same time, he didn't want any "stain" to tarnish his soul. The sacrament of Confession allowed him to obtain this goal: "Many little spots placed together will form a large one," Carlo said, "and in the end they blot out all the white space." Carlo prayed with the words of Psalm 51, the *Miserere*: "Wash me and I shall be whiter than snow.... Create in me a clean heart, O God, and put a new and right spirit within me."

When he taught catechism to children, he talked about a particular episode from the life of St. Anthony of Padua: "One day a great sinner came to him, having decided to change his life and make reparations for all the evil he had committed. He threw himself at the feet of the saint to make his Confession but wept so violently that he could not open his mouth, for tears of repentance wet his face. The holy friar then counseled him to go home and to write his sins on a piece of paper. The man obeyed and later returned with a long list. Friar Antonio read it out loud. He then gave the paper back to the penitent kneeling before him. How amazed was that repentant sinner when he saw the sheet was perfectly blank! Just as sins had disappeared from the soul of that sinner, so they did from the piece of paper as well!"[4]

Again, while teaching catechism to children younger than himself, he used a metaphor to describe the effects that our sins leave on our souls: "The smallest defect keeps us anchored to earth in the same way as balloons that are tied with a string held in our hand." Then, to explain the necessity of confessing often and well, he used another comparison: "To rise into the sky, a hot-air balloon has to unload weights. So too the soul, to rise into Heaven, has to remove the little weights called venial sins. If there is a mortal sin, the soul falls to the ground, and Confession is like the fire that makes the hot-air balloon climb once more into the sky. We must confess often because the soul is very complex."

Considering that he really loved flying kites on Mt. Subasio near Assisi and having his dogs run after him, it was easy for him to make another comparison as well: just as a kite needs the wind to take flight, so too our soul needs the Holy Spirit.

Another of Carlo's expressions reveals once more the importance he recognized of always being in a state of grace: "If people really realized the beauty of being in God's grace and respecting His commandments, they would do all they could not to commit grave sins and would do even more to help those who are living far from God." He would then quote St. Jacinta of Fatima, "If only people knew what eternity is, they would do everything to change their lives."[5]

Carlo saw that some of his friends and acquaintances consulted psychologists or coaches instead of going to Confession. These

---

[4] This story, told in Carlo's own words, is one of the many miracles attributed to St. Anthony of Padua. Cf. Ubaldus da Rieti, *St. Anthony of Padua* (Boston: Angel Guardian Press, 1895), 116.

[5] John de Marchi, *The True Story of Fatima: A Complete Account of the Fatima Apparitions* (Fatima Center, 2009), 70.

professionals, he told them, would of course listen to them, analyze them, and counsel them. But they would never propose conversion, i.e., changing one's life to orient it toward Jesus. Instead, they leave people to continue in their sin and distance themselves from God. The only solution that will truly make us happy is abandoning sin and beginning a new life in Christ through His sanctifying grace. The psychologist will shed light on difficulties, guilt complexes, and traumas but will never talk about sin, the relationship between man and God, and the love that God has given us that, because of sin, has been broken. Carlo knew that in the sacrament of Confession it is Christ at work, giving His mercy, giving us His Holy Spirit to reconcile us with the Church and with the Father, and bestowing the peace that only God can give, a sweet and imperturbable peace.

It was also important to him always to confess to the same priest so that he could better counsel him and in every Confession make very concrete proposals of conversion aiming at attainable goals.

A fundamental aspect of Carlo's life plan, thinking of when he made his First Communion, was reading and meditating on the Gospel. One of his favorite parables was that of the Sower (Matt. 13:4–23). It was important to him to make the seed bear a hundredfold and not allow the sprouted seeds to be suffocated by the thorns of life. He also really loved John 12, where Jesus, alluding to His approaching Passion, says, "Unless a grain of wheat falls into the earth and dies, it remains alone; but if it dies, it bears much fruit. He who loves his life loses it, and he who hates his life in this world will keep it for eternal life" (John 12:24–25).

During a weekday Mass one day, this Gospel passage was proclaimed. Immediately afterward, Carlo wrote the following:

> The more I'll be able to die to myself every day, the more I
> will be born again in Jesus. Jesus speaks of a grain falling to

the ground that, if it doesn't die, remains alone. We are all this grain of wheat, in the sense that we are all in a minimal position, like the seed. But we are such a precious seed that the Lord expects from it all that one can imagine.

We have within us a great resource called spirit or soul. It is our substantial component: we consist of soul and body. But our soul is simple, and what is simple cannot be broken down; it is not complex. Therefore, our soul is not made for time and space. At present, in this life, we are as it were closed in a trap, in a cage called time and space, on which we are dependent. Time and space make our existence difficult. But we have the spirit, which is simple and therefore immortal, and being immortal, has no need to remain in time and space. The kernel that we are, each one of us, is sown in the furrow to mature and develop and rise to the "level of the soul," being made neither for time nor space but for Eternity. But we are more than a grain of wheat, since we also have reason, so we need to collaborate with the development of this grain of wheat. To foster this development to allow the grain to become a whole head of wheat, we need to practice two virtues: humility and simplicity.

Humility is truth; humility is reality; humility does not consist in despising ourselves but in feeling ourselves below God. God and then us. Humility derives from the Latin word *humus*, which means earth. So the humble one is the one who comes from the earth, who is lowly and keeps a low profile. If we consider ourselves below God, we have found the proper proportion. And in proportion, we are humble. Humility makes us stay in our place. And it invites us and leads us to invigorate our resources and not spurn them, resources that we must cultivate for the glory of God.

Simplicity derives from the Latin *simplex*, which is composed of *sem* and *plicare*. *Sem* means "once" and *plicare* means "to bend or fold." The antonym of simple is complicated, which derives from the Latin *complicare* and means "to fold together." It is composed of the particle *cum* ("together") and *plicare* ("to bend or fold"). Therefore, complicated means being folded onto oneself, rendered less simple, to be confused, or difficult to understand.

Thus, simplicity is precisely the art of not being double, of not complicating, but of leaving everything on an open plane, at the disposal of God's glory and for the good of our brothers. Humility and simplicity are two virtues that allow the seed to leave the earth, to develop, and to become a head of wheat. This wheat becomes flour; the flour becomes bread; and the bread becomes the species or appearance needed for the Holy Eucharist. When Jesus speaks of a grain of wheat, He is thinking of Himself as the consecrated, transubstantiated Bread. And He is thinking of us as the people who live on this Bread and exist in this Bread and by means of this Bread are brought to Eternity. So we ask Jesus: *O God, make me a productive, efficient, efficacious grain of wheat. Jesus, make me a grain of wheat so that I can attain your eucharistic reality, of which I truly and really live.*

Along the same lines, there is another aspect of his program of conversion: the struggle against self-love, against pride, and on the positive side, the cultivation of humility. He was convinced that his Guardian Angel had suggested this beautiful phrase to him: "Not self-love, but the glory of God." The human ego, the ego closed in on itself, is the basis of pride and therefore the radical principle of every sin. Personal pride is the enemy of God because it challenges God's universal and absolute dominion. It is the enemy of men because it arouses interpersonal disputes and makes us irascible toward each other. It is the enemy of every individual man because it tempts us to stray from our true Good. The struggle against inordinate self-love is the constant task of every disciple of Jesus. Always trying to reduce the scope of pride is the start of the spiritual life and is also the beginning of our communion with Christ and our true peace. "Acting for the glory of God" means manifesting the qualities of God in our actions, above all His mercy.

But let's come back to humility. There is a text of Carlo's that reveals how decisive it always was [for him] to make reference to Jesus in matters of practical life:

Jesus wanted to place humility at the foundation of Christian asceticism. Humility is also the foundation of the other virtue He so often preached: charity. Humility is the virtue that allows us to live in society, that draws us together and converts us. What is humility? It is recognizing the good that is in God. It is recognizing all the evil that is in us and that we have done. The virtue of humility is a typically Christian virtue. Christ brought it to earth and was the first to live it.

Many say that Jesus was born poor, that He was placed in a manger, etc., and for that reason He was humble. But this is not what makes Jesus humble in His birth. Uniting human nature to His divine nature was the gesture of greatest humility. This is why He could say: "Learn from me, for I am meek and humble of heart" (Matt. 11:29, NABRE). After His baptism, Jesus was led into the desert for forty days. He let Himself be apprehended, bound, and pushed. No reaction. No opposition. No rebellion. He let Himself be taken. He was extraordinarily meek and submissive. It was all part of His plan. Throughout the entire span of His so-called public existence, during His various travels from one region to another — followed, chased, shoved, suspected, envied, attacked, insulted, doubted, abandoned — He carried out in full what He taught: *Learn from me for I am meek and humble of heart.* Meek and humble: gentle, sweet, available, modest, helpful, respectful, peaceful, calm, balanced, exemplary. The first capital vice, pride, had no sway over Him. He placed humility, a virtue almost unknown in previous history, at the root of His asceticism, as the basis of His morality, as the substance of His spirituality.

Learn from me, in other words imitate me, *for I am meek and humble of heart.* The heart, in Hebrew, signifies the mind, because the mind [*kilyah* in Hebrew, literally, the "kidneys,"] is the seat of our most profound decisions. *I love you with all my kidneys...* And God alone is the One who can scrutinize our most hidden affections and thoughts: "I am he who searches mind and heart, and I will give to each of you as your works deserve" (Rev. 2:23). Our decisions emanate from our hearts and our minds [kidneys], and these decisions will merit for us (or not) the reward of eternal life. The mind and heart are the seat of secret thoughts, of sensibilities, and of our hidden desires. All our thoughts have their origin in the heart, from which all our decisions emanate, both good and bad, and this is why Scripture exhorts us to guard our heart in innocence and to keep far from it all that is not pleasing to God. "Keep your heart with all vigilance; for from it flow the springs of life" (Prov. 4:23). Jesus also says, "There is nothing outside a man which by going into him can defile him; but the things that come out of him are what defile him" (Mark 7:15).

When God speaks to our heart it means He is speaking to our will, to our mind, to our conscience. For the Bible, the heart is the center of the person who makes decisions according to the will of God. In the book of the prophet Jeremiah, we read, "And I will give you shepherds after my own heart, who will feed you with knowledge and understanding" (3:15), and again, "Righteous art thou, O Lord, when I complain to thee" (12:1). We all ought to repeat this constantly! The desire to argue with God comes only from the Evil One. Therefore, being meek and humble of heart means we are humble of mind. Humility of mind is how we manifest the heart of the virtue invented by Jesus and practiced in His religion. The virtue of humility is the capacity to perceive evil in oneself and goodness in God. The capacity to not judge our neighbor but only judge ourselves. Indeed, this humility, descended from Heaven in Christ, is the fundamental, basic, and central virtue of Catholic spirituality: the humility that Jesus exercised in His Incarnation. The humility that He lived was not so much the fact of being born in a manger, but of passing through that exhausting corridor called Incarnation; in other words, Jesus was humble in associating the infinity of His [divine] substance to the finitude of His [human] condition. This exhausting passage of the Infinite to the finite was His humiliation. He gave us the continuous example of humility through His Incarnation during an entire generation, for more than thirty years, suffering and offering in a continuous exercise of humility.

Therefore, we Catholics need to decide to embrace humility, this fundamental virtue by which we bow before God and bow before our neighbor, and which deepens through charity, which is nothing other than humility in practice. Every lack of charity is a lack of humility, and vice versa. The world consists of pride. The essence of the world is arrogance. If we were truly humble, the Lord would bend down to us and grant us grace. Every grace withheld is an act of pride accomplished, and every grace granted is an act of humility accomplished. "Have this mind among yourselves, which was in Christ Jesus, who, though he was in the form of God, did not count equality with God a thing to be grasped, but emptied himself, taking the form of a servant, being born in the likeness of men. And being found in human form he humbled himself and became obedient unto death, even death on a cross. Therefore God has highly exalted him and bestowed on him the name which is above every name, that at the name of Jesus every knee should bow, in heaven and on Earth and under the earth, and every tongue confess that Jesus Christ is Lord, to the glory of God the Father" (Phil. 2:5–11).

Carlo remembered the terse words of Jesus, "If any man would come after me, let him deny himself and take up his cross daily and follow me" (Luke 9:23).

To gauge the extent to which we have reduced pride and grown in humility and interior freedom, Carlo suggested looking at the degree to which we endure criticism, both just and unjust. The more we are disturbed and angered by criticism received, the higher the level of our disordinate self-love and the longer the road we must walk to rid ourselves of pride, which is a serious obstacle in the path of sanctity.

Carlo was convinced that man, once he is freed of sin and from every disordered attachment, will be truly at peace and happy. He was always careful to make room for supernatural things in life and decided once and for all not to give too much importance to earthly things but to place his trust only in God. This was his plan for life.

#19

As regards detachment from the things of this world, Carlo understood quite well the difference between Christian detachment and a disdain, which is not a gospel attitude. Who were his teachers in this?

CARLO WAS ENTHUSIASTIC ABOUT life, about his parents, his grandparents, his friends, the people he knew, and the things he was involved in. He knew concretely that detachment from the things of this world, as Jesus taught, in no way meant hating or despising these things, as if they were antagonists to God. He was probably given a positive lesson in this from the words of the Trappist monk Thomas Merton, who wrote in *New Seeds of Contemplation*:

> Detachment from things does not mean setting up a contradiction between "things" and God as if God were another "thing" and as if His creatures were His rivals. We do not detach ourselves from things in order to attach ourselves to God, but rather we become detached *from ourselves* in order to see and use all things in and for God. This is an entirely new perspective which many sincerely moral and ascetic minds fail utterly to see. There is no evil in anything created by God, nor can anything of His become an obstacle to our union with Him. The obstacle is in our "self," that is to say in the tenacious need to maintain our separate, external, egotistical will. It is when we refer all things to this outward and false "self" that we alienate ourselves from reality and from God. It is then the false self that is our god, and we love everything for the sake of this self. We use all things, so to speak, for the worship of this idol that is our imaginary self. In so doing we pervert and corrupt things, or rather we turn our relationship to them into a corrupt and sinful relationship. We do not thereby make them evil, but we use them to increase our attachment to our illusory self.[6]

---

[6] Thomas Merton, *New Seeds of Contemplation* (Boston: Shambhala Publications, 1961), 23–24.

#20

"Faith apart from works is dead," as the apostle James writes in his canonical letter (2:26). We have already seen how Carlo lived charity toward God through participating in daily Mass, eucharistic adoration, and personal prayer. Could you tell us now how Carlo lived charity toward his neighbor outside of the family?

THERE ARE SO MANY anecdotes. Given the space available here, we have to limit them. The first memory in chronological order dates back to when Carlo was only five and a half years old. He had learned of the charitable organization "Work of St. Francis for the Poor" in Milan, directed by the Capuchins in Viale Piave. In particular, he encountered Fr. Giulio Savoldi, the assistant postulator and confessor of the venerable Br. Cecilio Maria Cortinovis, the porter friar who began this work, and he gave Fr. Savoldi all the money he had saved in his piggy bank, telling him it was for those most in need. Years later, Fr. Savoldi recalled this deed: he was touched that such a young child could be so generous. Even afterward, Carlo continued to frequent this charity for the poor and many remember him as a radiant child, very attentive to the needs of others, desiring to alleviate the pain and suffering of those less fortunate.

His nanny, Beata, who spent so much time with him, would also tell how, ever since he was very little, if he encountered a homeless person on the street, he would approach him with complete simplicity and speak to him and take interest in him, greeting him with his smile.

When he was older, he learned that the public shelters were often not large enough and confided to us his desire to start a charitable activity dedicated especially to the homeless. He imagined a large house in which every guest could have his own room.

We know much about his charitable works because he asked us for permission to buy things for the poor, like sleeping bags that he gave out personally to the homeless sleeping in the streets near our house in Milan. Or like the thermoses and insulated coolers. After buying them, he filled them with part of his dinner, with fruit, cookies, sandwiches, and sweets; then, together with our housekeeper Rajesh, he took them to the homeless who gathered around the Peace Arch next to Sempione Park, or in front of our parish Santa Maria Segreta. Using his own allowance and with our permission, he bought clothing and gave it to the homeless. He put into practice what St. Teresa of Calcutta would say: "You can do good right at home, without needing to journey somewhere."

He kept up these habits even when we were on vacation. For example, in Assisi once, when walking past the chapel of St. Stephen, he saw a person sleeping on the ground in a public park. That same evening after dinner, he took part of his dinner to him. And from that day on, he always asked Grandma Luana to prepare a bit extra so he could take it to that poor man. And sometimes he even left some money and not just his dinner.

Also when he went out to play with Mattia and Jacopo, his best friends in Assisi, if he met a poor person, he would stop and talk with him and would give him some money if he had any with him.

He gave not only food, clothing, or money to the poor, but he gave his attention, his words, his prayers. For example, when he was already in high school, he met an elderly, severely disabled person through the school and offered to visit her regularly. And so he did. He always brought her sweets, bought with his savings, and offered her comfort and affection.

In front of our parish in Milan, he met another elderly man, a beggar about eighty years old, who had no one to take care of him. He was suffering from diabetes and heart disease and thus was often in the hospital. Carlo asked us on numerous occasions if he could visit him in the hospital and take him what he needed for his hospital stay.

On another occasion, Carlo called us to ask permission to buy some groceries for two Gypsy children. Of course, we said yes. And so he accompanied them to the supermarket to do their shopping.

After Carlo's death, we met two people who begged in front of the parish because they could not find work. They told us how they were always amazed at Carlo's radiant smile. They remembered him with great fondness. Carlo treated them with great politeness and courtesy: even when he had nothing to give them, he stopped and spoke with them, concerned about their problems, their lives, and their future. And through his words, he was able to instill hope and courage. One of these beggars had mentioned to Carlo that Giuseppina (a homeless woman who stayed in the park in front of our parish) had fallen into depression and was letting herself die on the park bench. Strange bloodstains were already visible on her body. No one was looking after her. Carlo then asked us if he could help Giuseppina get medical help. Once we gave him permission, Carlo convinced Giuseppina to admit herself to the Fatebenefratelli Hospital. She spent more than forty days there. During her recovery, we went to visit her together. And when she was released, she was able to have government housing allocated to her.

A man of about fifty had lost his job and was begging on the steps of our parish in Milan. Carlo always met with him after weekday Mass, in the afternoon, and gave him some money and lingered to talk with him. In this way, he discovered that he needed a bicycle to get around more easily. Carlo immediately asked us if he could give him one. He had a special attentiveness to homeless people. He had begun to know them better by going to serve at the soup kitchen opened by the Sisters of Mother Teresa of Calcutta. Among the homeless, there were also many who were Muslims. Carlo made friends with them as well. And if they met on the street, in different contexts and on different occasions, they greeted one another with great warmth, and sometimes Carlo invited them to grab something to eat together.

All of this attention and concern toward the poor, the sick, and the suffering had one certain foundation: Carlo recognized in these people the actual, living presence of Jesus. He knew what Jesus says in Matthew 25, that the Lord Himself identifies with the thirsty, the hungry, the imprisoned, the needy. Christ is present in these people as the Crucified One.

When he gave a poor person a blanket, or a sleeping bag, or part of his dinner, his thoughts returned to the night of Jesus' birth, when everything was refused to Him. He wrote down:

> The Lord Jesus became incarnate, choosing a poor girl of only fifteen as His mother and a poor carpenter as His foster father. At His birth, He was rejected by the people who didn't know where to put Him and, in the end, someone found a stable for Him. If we really think about it, the stable in Bethlehem was certainly better than many homes today, where the Lord is still rejected and often even reviled because He is received in an unworthy manner. A poor girl of fifteen together with a poor carpenter were the parents of God, who chose poverty and not luxury.

He was helped in living out charity toward the poor by the example of two saints to whom he was very attached: St. Francis of Assisi and St. Anthony of Padua. And also by the courage of Don Oreste Benzi, the founder of the Pope John XXIII Community. Don Oreste, whose cause of canonization is underway, through his fraternal charity became a neighbor to the least among us: the sick, women fallen into trafficking, drug addicts. And Carlo considered him a "downright waterfall of light in a dark ocean during a storm."

Grandma Luana told us how one day she and Carlo, who was six at the time, were walking in Solari Park with our dog Chiara. Carlo enjoyed throwing sticks or rocks to have the dog retrieve them. At one point, another child approached and started playing with Carlo. They became friends. And Grandma Luana became friends with the boy's nanny. Some days later, the nanny showed up with her face covered in tears. Carlo noticed and asked her why. It turns out her parents in the Philippines had suffered a typhoon; their house had been destroyed, and her mother had broken bones throughout her body. The nanny was desperate, in part because she had no money to send to her parents. Before dinner, Carlo took his money from his piggy bank, asked us and Grandma Luana for more money, and quite happily gave the amount he had gathered to the nanny.

When he became an adolescent, with the money he had received as gifts and the money he had saved, he sponsored several children through a specialized pro-life association. In the summer of 2006, he was preparing to take a job the following summer in the municipal swimming pool in Assisi. In this way, he would gain direct work experience and learn the value of earning money; his plan was to collect more funds to help more needy people and adopt more children.

His charity was not limited to almsgiving but was shown through his attention to the other person and his or her needs. One of his favorite toys as a child was Legos. If he knew of a child who couldn't afford to buy a Lego set or other toys, he would immediately give him his own. As an adolescent, when he went swimming in the pool in Assisi, he offered to perform various services for the pool staff so that they could have time to take their lunch break.

Charity is not only doing but also bearing and forgiving offenses received. In this as well, Carlo is a splendid example for us. His friends knew that he attended Mass daily, and at times they made fun of him or even offended him. Likewise for his preference not to follow the latest fashions in clothing but to dress simply and without elegance. Carlo, as was his habit since infancy, did not react to their offenses but kept silent and endured it. He accepted humiliation and offered it to Jesus in prayer, knowing that Jesus Himself, true God and true Man, lived humility in silence, in a prayer of self-offering to the Father.

Charity is also helping and defending the weak. For Carlo it came naturally to take the side of the weak. Just as he came to the aid of the homeless, so too he helped a classmate who had problems with schoolwork or in using the computer, careful not to embarrass him. During afterschool hours, he was quite busy, without ever boasting or losing patience, but always with a smile. The judgments and teasing of others did not stop him; he continued to defend his companions who were disabled and took their side even in front of their teachers.

What follows is the testimony of the Jesuit Fr. Roberto Gazzaniga—at that time the principal of Leone XIII High School in Milan—testimony given during Carlo's process of beatification carried out by the Diocese of Milan:

> His attention toward those he perceived to be "sort of cutoff" dated already from that period. Some boys and girls need more time to get accustomed to the new context of school and classmates. From the very first days, Carlo drew near with discretion, respect, and courage to those who were struggling the most to find their place in the new reality of the class and the school. A few months after his parting from this earth and from his classmates, listening to

them and asking them about Carlo's character traits that had struck them, a number of them emphasized his sensitivity in perceiving from the very first day of school who was struggling most, and also his availability in approaching them and easing their integration into the class, encouraging them not to exasperate the situation and trying to break down resistance and silence. Many companions were grateful to Carlo for his ability to create and facilitate relations, to convey trust and solidarity without being intrusive.

Being present and making the other feel present was a detail that soon struck me about him. He gladly went through the hallways and the two floors of the high school during the longer morning break seeking out contact with other kids and teachers. He often had another classmate accompany him who otherwise would have stayed at his desk or have been alone waiting for the break to end. He had a respectful, vivacious, and very youthful ability to get things going and involve people. Various adults were amazed by his marked ability to take the initiative and by his courtesy, far from any excessive familiarity. The old doorman of the institute recalls Carlo's delicacy when some mornings he would enter through the side door, then would pass by the main door during the break just to say hi, not having done so in the morning. He did this spontaneously and would repeat the gesture with a constancy that was striking, given that typically students follow their mood swings when deciding whether to say hi.

Carlo's good nature, his search for direct contact, did not leave anyone indifferent. Being a pleasant boy, he created agreement and cohesion. It always amazed me that due to his innate qualities and abilities, he did not become the butt of jokes and pranks. Usually, when a student stands out above his peers, the others are very capable of "cutting him down to size" with barbs, allusions, and sneers. In a stage of life characterized by stark contradictions and competitiveness, it's not easy for an adolescent to recognize the superior value of a peer, the wealth of talents received and acquired. This is another element that speaks of Carlo's greatness in my eyes. The goodness and authenticity of his person won out over the games of revenge that tend to drag down to the lowest common denominator the reputation of those who are gifted with outstanding qualities.

His transparency was certainly a lived value. Carlo never hid his commitment to the Faith; even in conversations and verbal encounters or clashes with classmates, he maintained respect for the positions of others without ambiguity in saying and witnessing to the principles that inspired his Christian life. When one of my confreres entered Carlo's class to solicit participation in an extracurricular group called "Community of Christian Life CVX," Carlo came up to him immediately afterward telling him, "I'm interested in the evangelical initiative you spoke about." He was the only one in the whole class who took a position and declared his real interest in that communal proposal.

#21

The suffering of the innocent constitutes a scandal for some. In the face of tragedies that strike the innocent, especially children, some lose faith or start to doubt the goodness of God. How did Carlo live this relationship between innocent suffering and faith?

CARLO OFTEN SAID, "FROM birth, our earthly destiny is obvious: we are called to climb Golgotha and take up our cross." Each person's suffering is a participation in the *Via Crucis* of Jesus. This indeed is a mystery beyond our capacities that nevertheless reveals the immense love of

God for us. "Even though it cannot be fully comprehended," Carlo always said, "it has to be welcomed with gratitude and love. Once welcomed, this mystery will change and transform our heart and our life. It will help us understand what true love is according to God and keep us from being deceived by all those surrogates to love that the world presents us and that do no good to a person. The Word of God became man to give us back the grace we lost through Original Sin, and that we continue to lose every time we commit sin. Jesus could easily have brought to fulfillment His redeeming work in a painless manner. He did not lack means and systems and methods suitable for attaining the goal of salvation without having to turn to suffering. But no. He chose Calvary. He chose the Cross, humiliation, the Passion."

Faith in Christ, who died and rose again, revolutionizes our view of suffering, pain, and the tragic disasters of life: they become crosses, in other words, concrete means by which each Christian participates in his own little way in the events of Christ's salvation. Therefore, when seen in this way, if we accept them with faith and in union with Christ, these crosses become the cause of salvation for ourselves, for the souls in Purgatory, and for our neighbor for whom we pray.

Carlo regularly read a classic of Christian spirituality, *The Imitation of Christ*, where he found written that, "The whole life of Christ was a cross and a martyrdom."[7] Carlo developed this concept, stating that in the end, Jesus always suffered, from the moment He assumed human nature. Just think of the poverty of His life and His deprivations. First, the flight and exile into Egypt. Then His public life, riddled with death threats and continuous humiliations, without any privileges, but only schemes to condemn Him to death. And in the

---

[7]   Thomas à Kempis, *Imitation of Christ*, II.12, tr. Aloysius Croft and Harold Bolton (Milwaukee: Bruce Publishing Company, 1940).

end, the days of His Passion, the betrayal and the flight of His disciples, the arrest as if He were a brigand, the trials, the calumnies, the scorn, the flagellation and blood, and being nailed to the Cross. He could have saved us in another way. Why did He choose precisely this way? Only out of love for us. To Him, loving one's neighbor meant giving His life for him: "Greater love has no man than this, that a man lay down his life for his friends" (John 15:13). One who loves is ready to sacrifice his own existence for the beloved.

#22

How did Carlo develop such a Christian sense of pain and suffering?

PROBABLY THROUGH READING THE lives of the saints and their writings. For example, he knew the teaching of St. Ignatius of Loyola: "If God sends you many afflictions, it is a sign that He has great plans for you, and surely wants to make you a saint."[8] He was familiar with the popular story of St. Teresa of Avila who, as she was returning to her convent, was overtaken suddenly by a storm, tumbled off her horse and fell in the mud. With profound irony, she then turned to Jesus, saying, "If this is how you treat your friends, it is no wonder you have so few!"

---

[8] This popular synthesis of St. Ignatius's teaching draws on his voluminous correspondence. For example: "God our Lord has been visiting you with trials of body and soul, thus showing, in giving you so many occasions for merit, the very special love He has for you." Letter 4045 to Magdalene Angelica Domenech, January 12, 1554, in *Letters of St. Ignatius of Loyola*, trans. William J. Young (Chicago: Loyola University Press, 1959), 318.

Carlo was profoundly struck by the life experience of Blessed Alexandrina Maria da Costa. She received the stigmata and lived bedridden for fourteen years, eating only the Eucharist. The Lord appeared to her and gave her the mission to "suffer, love, make reparation."[9] Later, Our Lady encouraged her to accept this program of immolation. "Our Lady," said Alexandrina Maria, "has given me an even greater grace: first, abandonment; then, complete conformity to God's will; finally, the thirst for suffering."[10]

Carlo knew that the path that leads to the blessed life passes through a "narrow gate," as Jesus said (Matt. 7:13), and that everything works for our good if offered to God with faith and trust. He wrote,

> Mysteriously, every suffering bears two sides: the consequence of a prior disorder that caused it and the purifying action of God's mercy, perfectly united to His justice. God in His infinite wisdom has ordained that evil, the fruit of sin, which is rebellion against God, contributes to the good of those who love Him, by means of their purification and sanctification.

Carlo saw God's mercy as closely united to His justice, both of them redeeming man from the consequences of his sin. God does not abandon man in his disordinate condition; He does not leave him alone but continuously knocks on his heart to give him His grace and peace.

To understand something of the mystery of suffering, Carlo always quoted Scripture: "For one is approved if, mindful of God, he

---

9 As cited in John Paul II, "Homily for the Beatification of Six Servants of God" (April 25, 2004), no. 7, https://www.vatican.va/content/john-paul-ii/en/homilies/2004/documents/hf_jp-ii_hom_20040425_beatifications.html.

10 *Alexandrina Maria da Costa* (1904-1955), Vatican News Services, https://www.vatican.va/news_services/liturgy/saints/ns_lit_doc_20040425_da-costa_en.html.

endures pain while suffering unjustly" (1 Pet. 2:19). Or he recalled the prophecy of the Suffering Servant of Yahweh: "By his knowledge shall the righteous one, my servant, make many to be accounted righteous; and he shall bear their iniquities. Therefore I will divide him a portion with the great, and he shall divide the spoil with the strong; because he poured out his soul to death, and was numbered with the transgressors; yet he bore the sin of many, and made inter-cession for the transgressors" (Isa. 53:11–12). The Suffering Servant of Yahweh takes away "the sin of the world" (John 1:29), of which sickness is only the consequence. The prophet Isaiah, who lived al-most six hundred years before the Passion of Christ, announces something magnificent: the suffering of the Just One gives salvation to all and eliminates even the sins of others. This prophecy was ful-filled in the Passion and Death of Jesus on the Cross. Only the Passion of Jesus revolutionizes the meaning of suffering, redeems it, by making it His own and making it the cause of eternal salvation for all His disciples. Here we must quote paragraph 1473 of the *Catechism*:

> The forgiveness of sin and restoration of communion with God entail the remission of the eternal punishment of sin, but temporal punishment of sin remains. While patiently bearing sufferings and trials of all kinds and, when the day comes, serenely facing death, the Christian must strive to ac-cept this temporal punishment of sin as a grace. He should strive by works of mercy and charity, as well as by prayer and the various practices of penance, to put off completely the "old man" and to put on the "new man" (Eph. 4:22, 24).

#23

Jesus taught in His first public discourse, "When you pray, you must go into your room and shut the door and pray to your Father who is in secret; and your Father who sees in secret will reward you" (Matt. 6:6). Can you share with us something about how Carlo prayed?

CARLO HAD AN ICON in his room in Milan, a reproduction of the Mother of God of Vladimir. He was very attached to it because he said that it is possible to dialogue with icons. Carlo was familiar with the teaching of St. John Damascene concerning icons. And so he knew they were not mere paintings but " filled with energy and divine grace."[11] They are like a prolongation of the [Mystical] Body of Christ, i.e., the humanity of Christ glorified, together with our humanity in the communion of saints. Christ glorified and the saints transmit something of their holiness through the physical matter of the icon. Icons are, therefore, a sort of theophany, a manifestation of God and the saints whom they represent. They are a window that gives us access to the beauty of the divine communion that awaits us in fullness in Heaven. Carlo loved to pray in silence before this icon, just as he loved to retreat into the hills of Assisi to pray in silence. He did not seek to escape from the world, but rather from the distractions of the world, in order to listen to the voice of God, to meditate on His Word. Occasionally he told us, "Prayer is the language of Heaven," meaning the mutual love of the Most Holy Trinity. And remaining united to this Love that is God was enough for him.

---

[11] John Damascene, *Three Treatises on the Divine Images* 1.16, tr. Andrew Louth (Crestwood: St. Vladimir's Seminary Press, 2003), 29.

He would also say, "As our capacity to love gradually increases, we become ever more upright and pure. And we shall be able to say with a free soul: God is my 'all.' On our own, we are incapable of adding even just one hour to our life, nor could we ever procure for ourselves the grace we need, but we must always ask God for it. Praying makes us see everything from the viewpoint of Eternity. And the difficulties of this world will seem like nothing to us if we view them from that perspective."

Carlo considered vocal prayers a very efficacious means for being united to God. For Carlo, plunging himself in God through recollection and prayer was like entering into Heaven through a door and sitting down at his place in Eternity.

He had a predilection for the Holy Rosary: every day he recited five mysteries. Carlo would recite them separately as well, while going to school, or on the bus, while going for walks, or at home after dinner. Through the Rosary he united two important aspects: vocal prayer and mental prayer, namely the meditation of the salvific events of the life of Jesus. We already discussed how Carlo took imitation of Jesus' life as his point of reference. The Rosary helped him to observe and meditate on some of the moments of Jesus' life through the gaze of Mary who, as we read in Luke 2:19, "kept all these things," namely the events concerning the life of Jesus, "pondering them in her heart."

Meditating on the event of the Annunciation of the angel to Mary, he said that "in welcoming the message of the angel who announced the birth of the Savior, Mary's yes gave us the ideal icon on which to model our lives." The Rosary teaches us various methods of prayer: meditation and the litany-like repetition of the Hail Mary. This union allows the events of salvation from the life of Jesus to descend from the mind to the mouth and then to the heart. And that rhythm of vocal prayer elevates our mind to God, while considering the events of Jesus' life helps us to avoid distractions and to meditate on a passage of the Gospel.

He knew that the ideal would be to recite the Rosary together with others or in church. In fact, the Church grants a plenary indulgence (the forgiveness of the temporal punishments due to our sins) to those who recite five mysteries of the Rosary either alone in church or with others even when not in a church, on the condition that the person is in God's grace, goes to Confession and receives the Eucharist within eight days,[12] prays for the intentions of the pope, and has the interior disposition of detachment from all sin, even venial. But if he was not able to recite the Rosary in church or with others, Carlo took into account the advice that St. Pio of Pietrelcina gave to one of his spiritual daughters, Margherita Cassano. She had come to him with the dilemma: "Father, they told me that prayer in common is worth more than prayer recited alone, according to what Jesus said: 'Where two or three are gathered in my name, there am I in the midst of them' (Matt. 18:20). But I recite the Rosary alone at home, alone in the street, alone at my job." And Padre Pio replied, "And why would you not recite the Rosary with your Guardian Angel? Entrust to him the 'Hail Mary, etc.,' and you take the 'Holy Mary, etc.' As St. Luke tells us, the Hail Mary is God's greeting to Mary placed in the mouth of an angel, and so it is a good and lovely thing for the angels to say it too."[13] Thus, when he was alone, Carlo

---

[12] The Apostolic Penitentiary's document *Gift of the Indulgence* (January 29, 2000) specifies that the traditional obligation of Confession and sacramental Communion "within several days" should be understood to mean *about twenty days* before or after doing an indulgenced work; https://www.vatican.va/roman_curia/tribunals/apost_penit/documents/rc_trib_appen_pro_20000129_indulgence_en.html.

[13] Translated from Marcello Stanzione, "Le missioni notturne dell'angelo custode di Padre Pio," *Aleteia*, November 4, 2020, https://it.aleteia.org/2020/11/04/missioni-notturne-angelo-custode-di-padre-pio.

imitated Margherita Cassano: he recited the Rosary invoking his Guardian Angel.

He was also familiar with the fifteen promises that Mary made in 1464 to Alan de la Roche, a Dominican friar in France, who later became a great preacher and promoter of the prayer of the Rosary:

1. Those who faithfully serve me by the recitation of the Rosary shall receive signal graces.

2. I promise my special protection and the greatest graces to all those who shall recite the Rosary.

3. The Rosary shall be a powerful armor against Hell. It will destroy vice, decrease sin, and defeat heresies.

4. The recitation of the Rosary will cause virtue and good works to flourish. It will obtain for souls the abundant mercy of God. It will withdraw the hearts of men from the love of the world and its vanities, and it will lift them to the desire of eternal things. Oh, that souls would sanctify themselves by this means.

5. The soul which recommends itself to me by the recitation of the Rosary shall not perish.

6. Those who recite my Rosary devoutly, applying themselves to the consideration of its sacred mysteries, shall never be conquered by misfortune. In his justice, God will not chastise them; nor shall they perish by an unprovided death, i.e., be unprepared for Heaven. Sinners shall convert. The just shall persevere in grace and become worthy of eternal life.

7. Those who have a true devotion to the Rosary shall not die without the sacraments of the Church.

8. Those who faithfully recite the Rosary shall have, during their life and at their death, the light of God and the plenitude of his graces. At the moment of death, they shall participate in the merits of the saints in paradise.

9. I shall deliver from Purgatory those who have been devoted to the Rosary.

10. The faithful children of the Rosary shall merit a high degree of glory in Heaven.

11. By the recitation of the Rosary you shall obtain all that you ask of me.

12. Those who propagate the Holy Rosary shall be aided by me in their necessities.

13. I have obtained from my Divine Son that all the advocates of the Rosary shall have for intercessors the entire celestial court during their life and at the hour of their death.

14. All who recite the Rosary are my beloved children and the brothers and sisters of my only Son, Jesus Christ.

15. Devotion for my Rosary is a great sign of predestination.[14]

---

[14] *Rosary Center & Confraternity,* https://rosarycenter.org/confraternity-obligations-benefits-and-promises.

Carlo's predilection for the Rosary grew even more after our first pilgrimage to Fatima. In the apparition on August 19, 1917, Mary invited the three young visionaries to pray and offer sacrifices: "Pray, pray very much, and make sacrifices for sinners; for many souls go to hell, because there are none to sacrifice themselves and to pray for them."[15] Carlo took these words literally and realized he was not offering enough sacrifices and prayers for those who were far from God. He even dreamed about one of the visionaries, Francisco, who asked Carlo to make reparations with personal prayer and sacrifices so that the faithful would love the Eucharist more. A few days after the death of Sr. Lucia in 2005, Carlo encountered her in a dream; she confided to him that through the practice of the First Five Saturdays, every believer could change the destiny of the world. He often said, "After the Holy Eucharist, the Holy Rosary is the most powerful weapon for fighting the devil and is the shortest ladder for climbing to Heaven."

Carlo read the Letter of the apostle James in which he teaches the importance of the prayer of intercession for others: "The prayer of a righteous man has great power in its effects. Elijah was a man of like nature with ourselves and he prayed fervently that it might not rain, and for three years and six months it did not rain on the earth. Then he prayed again and the heaven gave rain, and the earth brought forth its fruit. My brethren, if any one among you wanders from the truth and someone brings him back, let him know that whoever brings back a sinner from the error of his way will save his soul from death and will cover a multitude of sins" (5:16–20).

Convinced of all this, Carlo prayed for his friends and entrusted them to God, especially those who used drugs, who got drunk, and who wasted entire evenings at discos. They would often invite him to

---

[15] Sr. Lucia of Fatima, *Fatima in Lucia's Own Words*, 16th ed., ed. Louis Kondor (Secretariado dos Pastorinhos, 2007), 93.

join them, but Carlo told us that he would rather follow the advice of his Guardian Angel not to go, and instead to pray for his friends and ask the prayers of monks and nuns for them as well.

Besides the prayers of consecrated men and women, Carlo considered the prayers of parents for their children to be very important: "If one day as these kids grow up, they were to stray from the path that leads to God, sooner or later the Lord will remember the prayers they recited together as a family and will guide them back into the sheepfold." The prayers of a father or a mother, offered in sincerity, faith, and devotion, are always heard by God, who will grant them at the opportune moment.

#24

You recalled Carlo's phrase "After the Holy Eucharist, the Holy Rosary is the most powerful weapon." What was the relation between the Eucharist and Carlo's prayer?

IF WE WERE TO omit the Eucharist, both as a celebrated sacrament (the Mass) and as the real, permanent presence of Christ in the tabernacle, we would be incapable of understanding anything about Carlo's life.

Carlo's spiritual life was lived within the eucharistic mystery.

As a little boy, when he spent his afternoons with Beata, he went with her to Mass, since she was in the habit of going to daily Mass. He went along gladly, although at his age he was not able to receive Communion. Later, he made his First Communion at age seven on June 16, 1998, after which he continued going to daily Mass with even greater enthusiasm and adored the Eucharist either before or after Mass.

The day of his First Communion he was delighted, radiant, and he told us his intention: "To be always united to Jesus, this is my life's mission." And Carlo certainly surrendered himself to the Eucharist to grow in sanctifying grace and, in this way, behold the gates of Heaven wide open. The centrality that he acknowledged in the Eucharist was most likely inspired in him by the marked eucharistic spirituality of the nuns of Perego. He received his First Communion in their church and in the presence of their community. A few days later he wrote,

> The more Eucharists we receive the more we shall become similar to Jesus and, already on this earth, we shall have a foretaste of Paradise.

He considered himself very fortunate: "If we think about it," he said, "we are so much more fortunate that those who lived more than two thousand years ago alongside Jesus in Palestine. The apostles, the disciples, the people of that time could meet Him, touch Him, speak to Him, but they were still limited by time and space. Many had to travel great distances to encounter Him, though it wasn't always possible to approach Him because He was always surrounded by crowds. Think of Zaccheus who had to climb a tree to see Him. For us, we just have to go down to the nearest church and we have 'Jerusalem' next door! The people who lived next to Jesus could not eat His Body and drink His Blood like we can. They could not make eucharistic adoration through which Jesus transfigures us and assimilates us more and more to Himself. He is the one who told us, 'You, therefore, must be perfect, as your heavenly Father is perfect' (Matt. 5:48). Hiding Himself in the Eucharist, He gives us His entire being — His Body and Blood, Soul and Divinity — and helps us to bring about our sanctification. Jesus invites us to go to Him: 'If any one thirst, let him come to me and drink. He who believes in me, as the scripture has said, *Out of his heart shall flow rivers of living water'* (John 7:37–38). If people only understood the importance of the Eucharist, there would be such long lines to receive Communion that we would no longer be able to enter the churches."

For Carlo, the Eucharist was the most supernatural reality because in it, God makes Himself present, and at the same time, it is the reality most easily accessible to everyone: it is the real sign of His benevolence toward us.

#25

Carlo's phrase "The Eucharist is the highway to Heaven" went around the world. Do you remember other things Carlo said about the Eucharist?

CARLO WAS IN LOVE with this sacrament and spoke about it often. For example, he told us, "The sacraments are not seven, but six plus one. Six give or restore grace. One, the Eucharist, is the fountain of grace. Therefore 'in' and 'with' and 'through' this sacrament, the more one receives it, the more grace is poured into us. The various prayers, novenas, pilgrimages, and weeks for Christian unity without the Eucharist are merely 'hot air.'" With simple and familiar words such as these, Carlo made his own the words of St. Thomas Aquinas: "The Eucharist is the end and consummation of all the sacraments." "All the other sacraments seem to be ordained to this one [the Eucharist] as to their end." "The graces of all the sacraments prepare us to receive or to consecrate the Eucharist."[16]

At other times, Carlo said things like:

> "To receive more grace, one must be assiduous in the sacrament of the Eucharist."

> "Each of us needs to conform himself to Communion. Namely, we must make a daily effort to improve ourselves. How? Removing one defect after another and acquiring one virtue after another. The entire secret lies in this. If over 951 years have passed since the Schism of the East, and over 488 years since the Protestant rebellion, this has happened because men sought to study too much theology and too much history, but have not sought to become saints."

> "The plan of God's goodness is that grace circulate in such a way that Christians of the three confessions feel the push toward unity. The daily life of Christians must be substantially and essentially characterized by this augmentation, this amassing, this capitalization of grace. All the rest is marginal or, at best, doesn't add all that much."

Carlo said that if eucharistic adoration is adoring God, then we find in it the whole of creation. He knew that by adoring the Eucharist for at least half an hour one could obtain a plenary indulgence according to the conditions established by the Church (as we saw for reciting the Rosary) and that one could apply the indulgence to oneself or to the souls in Purgatory. And he said that, although the main condition required is quite difficult to live, namely having no affection for sin,

---

[16] Thomas Aquinas, *Summa Theologica*, III Q. 63, a. 6; Q. 65, a. 3; and Q. 73, a. 3.

not even venial sin, we should not despise the grace of forgiveness and the indulgence granted in virtue of the merits of Jesus Christ, the saints, and the power that Jesus conferred to Peter to bind and loosen sins (cf. Matt. 16:19).

Carlo also shared with us his interpretation of the last phrase that Jesus pronounced in the Gospel according to Matthew: "Lo, I am with you always, to the close of the age" (28:20). He liked to say, "*With you* means existence for two. *With* means life together. And life together means living together, sharing together, working together; it means plans for two, interaction, organizational harmony, questions and answers, joint activities, connatural ideas, ideals pursued together, values defended together, values improved together. *With you* means the tabernacle of mutual understanding, of mutual support, of working together. The words *with you* must be turned into life. And they are turned into life if inside there is Life. Becoming conscious of the tabernacle, reacquainting ourselves with the tabernacle, taking care of the tabernacle, being good stewards of the tabernacle, we fulfill the *with you*. For God's creatures endowed with reason, the trinitarian program is clear: elevation to the supernatural state, adoption as sons, inheritance of co-eternity. God said to Moses: 'I will be with you' (Exod. 3:12), and Jesus Christ repeats it to each one of us, baptized in His name, who seeks to live observing His Gospel."

Carlo was so convinced of all this that he organized his days by placing the daily encounter with Jesus in the sacrament of the Eucharist in the center, participating in Mass and adoring Him in the tabernacle.

Among his various notes (though we do not know if they are a transcription of a meditation he heard or his personal thoughts), we read the following, all centered on the fact that the triune God has been living among us for the past two thousand years:

"And the Word became flesh"—assuming human nature, associating it with the divine nature in one Divine Person—"and dwelt among us" (John 1:14). But the word *dwell* should not be understood in the common sense of taking up residency, residing, making a home on this earth. It is not this. When we use the term *dwell* in our language, we are instinctively led to think of something like: he has taken up residence in a certain place. This term *dwell* can lead to alarmingly reductive conclusions. The verb *dwell*, or *inhabit*, comes from the Latin *habere*, which means "to have," but which has many other auxiliary meanings. It also signifies to hold, to frequent, to possess, to sanctify, to assimilate, to become second nature, to pair, and many other things. Therefore, we must take this phrase "dwelt among us" as meaning something much more general, more universal, broader, infinitely broader; and so when Scripture says "and the Word became flesh and dwelt among us" the words taken alone do not convey the whole breadth of meaning contained in the inspired word of John the evangelist who, writing under the influence of the Holy Spirit, meant to say many things.

When Jesus assumed human nature, he became Man, he descended to this planet, not as an extraterrestrial but as One who, dwelling outside time and space, entered time and space in that nature and subsumed it, assimilated it, became second nature with it, was paired with it. And so, Jesus became, as the apostle Paul says, "all in all" (Col. 3:11), embracing the realism of this planet, its true substantiality—this planet Earth that is part of creation and therefore of the universe. Before the Incarnation, humanity was prisoner of original and actual sin and throughout the centuries was heading toward an abyss that seemed unfathomable, insurmountable. But, at a certain point, "Love" prevailed over "Justice," "Mercy" prevailed over "Punishment," and sin was defeated by the Incarnation. ... This planet that was able to see in You, for one generation, the second Person of the Most

Holy Trinity incarnate, for twenty centuries now is not the same one as before. Yes, astronomically, scientifically, geologically, it might be the same as before, but from the gospel point of view, that of the Incarnation, it is not the same as before; it is a planet that has been subsumed by Eternity in a divine plan in which we have been truly inserted for over twenty-one centuries. We have to think of this so-called *dwelling* as an appropriation of the planet by Jesus and realize that Jesus—who still dwells in the Eucharist and by faith among us, and therefore walks in our midst—lives in our midst, sharing with us our daily life, both in the Eucharist and in faith, and so we must see this habitation as a true dwelling of Christ on this planet Earth. We see Jesus among us; we see Jesus with us; we see Jesus truly in us.

And so the Eucharist, this "second Incarnation," truly comes into being, not so much as a sacrament in the ritual sense, but in a supernatural sense. For this reason, when we receive Communion, Jesus who dwells with us for fifteen minutes hidden under the species of bread and wine, substantially present, truly dwells in the sense I explained before, in other words, shares our daily life with us and continues, even after the species of bread and wine have dissolved, to dwell with us through His grace. And so, we become His house, His dwelling. In this Jesus, present, living, and true within us, is not merely a matter of faith, not merely a matter of "sacramentality," but is a fact of Life! In other words, Jesus is with me and I am with Him—an extremely personal, individual fact. This direct contact between me and Jesus occurs by means of the Eucharist and faith. When Jesus came to planet Earth, He sought to summarize, or as Paul says, "recapitulate" (cf. Eph. 1:10) in Himself all Eternity, all humanity: humanity before Him, humanity during His earthly life, and humanity after Him. This is what it means to dwell. And Jesus, dwelling in this way, reassumed in Himself, day after day, hour after hour, the whole human race, in all its aspects. And so we stand before a miracle that truly leaves us in awe and amazement. It is the miracle of redemption, it is the miracle of the life of Jesus with us, which recapitulated all humanity in Himself and rendered Him truly, really the Redeemer, Savior, Sanctifier of each of us.

"Through the Eucharist we shall be transformed into Love," Carlo would always say. "As bread and wine through their Consecration, by the power of the Holy Spirit, become the Body and Blood of Christ, in the same way we too will be 'transubstantiated' in Christ." He drew this assurance from his meditation of John 6:

> Jesus reassures us: "I am the bread of life" (John 6:35); "I am the living bread which came down from heaven" (6:51). And He repeats with authority that "it was not Moses who gave you the bread from heaven; my Father gives you the true bread from heaven" (6:32). Jesus is the true Living Bread come down from Heaven that shall never perish, unlike that which the people of Israel ate in the desert, the manna, which is bread that perishes (cf. 6:49–51). When Jesus says that "it was not Moses who gave you the bread from heaven," but that it is His Father who gives the true Bread of Heaven, He is introducing the Eucharist. His great plan, His prestigious plan, His prodigious plan is taking shape, is becoming a reality. He introduces the Father as the one who gives the true Bread and defines Himself as *the Bread of God*. Here we enter the setting of the Eucharist.
>
> "The one who comes down from heaven" — this is an expression that must be written down, meditated upon, studied, and contemplated. Heaven is Eternity. Descent is spoken of because Heaven is considered an entity above us, but the term merely signifies 'coming' or 'arriving' from Eternity into time, and from the realm beyond spatial dimensions into our earthly conditioning. It signifies the

Most Holy Trinity intervening in a totally unique way with rational beings. An encounter takes place.

The "Bread of God"—i.e., Life. "And so they said to him, 'Lord, give us this bread always'" (6:34). And Jesus responds, "I am the bread of life; he who comes to me shall not hunger, and he who believes in me shall never thirst" (6:35). Here Jesus declares in an unequivocal and unavoidable manner that he is "the bread of life." *Bread* defines him. And *of life* clarifies. His plan is taking shape through His words. He is promising to be 'nourishment.' If we think about it, this is astounding. It is a historical event. The expression "I am the bread of life" means that the abnormal and enormous weight [of nourishing the world] has been assumed by Christ, is born by the divine nature, is rendered entirely celestial by the Divine Person, in order that we not hunger or thirst anymore. Christ is really and substantially present under the species or appearance of bread and wine. He is the Bread that gives existence its breakthrough into the Beyond.

Then Jesus adds, "But I said to you that you have seen me and yet do not believe" (John 6:36). He accuses them of lack of faith. They mutter about the unusual expression, "I am the bread which came from heaven" (6:41). They fall back on their knowledge of His geographical origins. They know Mary and Joseph. Here we have a precious demonstration or proof of the historicity of Jesus. For them it is something odd, absurd, that doesn't hold water. They clearly heard Him say: "I am the bread come from heaven." What kind of bread is that? What Heaven is He talking about? What is this coming from Heaven all about? And they argue and rave and speculate. It is almost anguishing. Jesus confronts them: "Do not murmur among yourselves. No one can come to me unless the Father who sent me draws him; and I will raise him up at the last day.... Truly, truly, I say to you, he who believes has eternal life" (6:43–44, 47). So Jesus brings them back to the level of the supernatural.

He then explains: "If anyone eats of this bread, he will live forever; and the bread which I shall give for the life of the world is my flesh" (John 6:51). He tells them His will: He wants to give food and drink. He does not theorize. He does not entrench Himself in the Absolute. He does not complicate the matter with abstract reasoning. He speaks of manna, of the desert, of the fathers, of death. They cannot contest Him about this. The Bible is there in the synagogue, and everyone can read and remember it. But then, like lightning in a clear sky, He adds that He is the Living Bread that ensures Eternity. He speaks of His flesh for the life of the world. This is His physio-psychic-spiritual reality. This reality is the Bread of life, the bread we must eat if we want to live eternally. Otherwise, eternal death. He threw a boulder into the pond: this great, enormous, stunning declaration, affirmation, promise. He spoke so clearly, and expressed Himself in such precise and unequivocal terms, that the Jews then disputed among themselves, saying, "How can this man give us his flesh to eat?" (6:52). They understood perfectly well. They are almost accusing Him of promoting cannibalism. *Flesh to eat*: they focused on this.

Admittedly, the affirmations and declarations of Jesus are not in the least predictable. They are explosive. They tear open the heavens. But Jesus replies, "Truly, truly, I say to you, unless you eat the flesh of the Son of man and drink his blood, you have no life in you; he who eats my flesh and drinks my blood has eternal life, and I will raise him up at the last day. For my flesh is food indeed, and my blood is drink indeed. He who eats my flesh and drinks my blood abides in me, and I in him. As the living Father sent me, and I live because of the Father, so he who eats me will live because of me. This is the bread which came down from heaven, not such as the fathers ate and died; he who eats this bread will live forever" (John 6:53–58). The center of gravity is found in these six verses. These six verses are magnetic, for they speak of the Beyond; they point to

Eternity. They do not speak in generic or approximate terms. They do not drag out the discussion into long-winded arguments. Nor do they dance around the point. Jesus immediately and concretely asks them to be nourished by Him, otherwise they will not have life. He offers Himself to us as food and drink. He wants us to be nourished by Him. His divine-human reality is placed at our complete and total and comprehensive disposition. If this is not love, what could it possibly be? Jesus actualizes an intimate bond with Him, a bond on a vital level. A bond that leads to Eternity. Jesus and us. Jesus with us. Jesus through us. Jesus in us. He is visibly wanting to create an interpersonal relationship with us.

This invitation to conviviality is addressed to each individual man, each individual woman. Eating and drinking mean ingesting our daily food and drink. Ingesting means introducing into our organism. Until the species or appearances of bread and wine dissolve, we have within us the presence of the Body and Blood, Soul and Divinity of Christ. Our living organism is intimately bound to Jesus Christ, true God and true Man. Jesus promises eternal life to those who receive Communion. He does not say *will have*, but *has* eternal life. Life that is eternal, therefore, co-eternity. In Communion we have eternal life. Having eternal life means, and is, possessing everything necessary and indispensable to enter and be part of co-eternity. One is enrolled in the "registry of Heaven." One is, with full rights, a citizen of co-eternity.

And Jesus insists, "For my flesh is food indeed, and my blood is drink indeed" (John 6:55). He gives everything. And again, "He who eats my flesh and drinks my blood abides in me, and I in him" (6:56). He who receives Communion, comes home. A home that is co-inhabited. Together under the same roof. *In Me* and *in Him*: this is more than cohabitation; the two are fused together, united. This union is not symbolic or poetic or sentimental. What is it then? Evidently, it indicates a relationship that is the opposite of *outside* or *near*. It is a reality that touches the roots, that reaches the depths, that plunges into intimacy. Jesus wants to realize and carry out this union through giving us His Body and Blood, Soul and Divinity.

And He finishes by saying: "As the living Father sent me, and I live because of the Father, so he who eats me will live because of me. This is the bread which came down from heaven, not such as the fathers ate and died; he who eats this bread will live forever" (John 6:57–58). Jesus, the Revealer of the Trinity, presents the Trinity to us in its absolute unity. And he indicates their names: Father, Son, Holy Spirit. The Father begets. The Son is begotten. The Holy Spirit proceeds from the Father and from the Son. Through them we have existence. And through Communion, this blossoms into life. Jesus speaks of life, promises life, gives life. This life is the Eucharist. The Eucharist is Christ, true Man and true God. The Bread of life is Christ. He is the Bread come down from Heaven. From Eternity into time. From Heaven to planet Earth. Descending, taking Himself from up there to down here. Communion is the substantial and abundant injection of life into our existence. In conclusion: Jesus makes himself substantially present in Body, Blood, Soul, and Divinity under the species or appearances of bread and wine. The Council of Trent speaks of 'transubstantiation.' After Consecration, only the accidents of the bread and wine remain—their color, taste, scent, and quantity. [The Eucharist is] bread and wine in its accidents, but Jesus in substance.

#26

I shall address Antonia. You already recalled how Carlo came up with the idea and participated in the execution of the book Eucharistic Miracles *and the* Christian Roots of Europe. *He also collaborated on* The Little Eucharistic Catechism, *which deals in a simple way with transubstantiation.*

CARLO WAS FASCINATED BY the mystery of transubstantiation. This consists in the fact that through the celebration of the sacrament, what is bread becomes the Body of Christ and what is wine becomes the Blood of Christ. And in light of this transition, Jesus Christ is present in the species of bread and wine, not in terms of quantity, or the superficial manner of extension, but in terms of substance. For example, I am still myself whether as a child or now as an adult; my substance as a human being has not grown in proportion to my bodily growth. My humanity does not grow in terms of its substance, nor does it diminish as my age or height does. Human substance remains the same in me. In a similar way, Jesus is substantially present in the Eucharist, not according to the greater or lesser dimensions of the surface of the consecrated Host, but according to His substance as the Word incarnate, a substance that remains always the same and is not subject to increase or decrease.

To meditate on these truths more easily, Carlo transcribed some quotes from the saints. For example, this passage of St. John Chrysostom, commenting on Ephesians 5:30 (NKJV): "We are members of his body, of his flesh, and of his bones":

> In order then that we may become this not by love only, but in very deed, let us be blended into that flesh. This is

effected by the food which He hath freely given us, desiring to show the love which He hath for us. On this account He hath mixed up Himself with us; He hath kneaded up His body with ours, that we might be a [one] like a body joined to a head. ... He hath given to those who desire Him not only to see Him, but even to touch, and eat Him, and fix their teeth in His flesh, and to embrace Him, and satisfy all their love. Let us then return from that table like lions breathing fire.... Parents often entrust their offspring to others to feed; "but I," saith He, "do not so, I feed you with Mine own flesh, for your sake I shared in flesh and blood [in the Incarnation], and in turn I give out to you the flesh and the blood by which I became your kinsman." [17]

To meditate on the real and true presence of Jesus in the Eucharist, he wrote down a passage from the commentary of St. Thomas Aquinas on John 6:56:

For my flesh is meat indeed, and my blood is drink indeed. Some might think that what he was saying about his flesh and blood was just an enigma and a parable. So our Lord rejects this, and says, *my flesh is meat indeed.* As if to say: do not think that I am speaking metaphorically, for my flesh is truly contained in this food of the faithful, and my blood is truly contained in this sacrament of the altar: *This is my body.... This is my blood of the New Covenant* (Matt. 26:26)....

He who eats my flesh and drinks my blood abides in me, and I in him. Here our Lord shows that this spiritual food has such power, that is, to give eternal life. And he reasons this way: whoever eats my flesh and drinks my blood is

[17] John Chrysostom, *Homilies on the Gospel According to John*, 46.3. https://www.documentacatholicaomnia.eu/03d/0345-0407,_Iohannes_Chrysostomus,_Homilies_on_The_Gospel_Of_John,_EN.pdf.

united to me, but whoever is united to me has eternal life: therefore, whoever eats my flesh and drinks my blood has eternal life....

There is another way by which those who eat do not abide in Christ nor Christ in them. This is the way of those who approach with an insincere heart: for this sacrament has no effect in one who is insincere. There is insincerity when the interior state does not agree with what is outwardly signified. In the sacrament of the Eucharist, what is outwardly signified is that Christ is united to the one who receives it, and such a one to Christ. Thus, one who does not desire this union in his heart, or does not try to remove every obstacle to it, is insincere. Consequently, Christ does not abide in him nor he in Christ.[18]

Carlo also copied down this summary of Thomas Aquinas's thought: "All the sacraments operate in virtue of the Passion of Our Lord Jesus Christ."[19] The sacrifice of Jesus, His offering in love to the Father for our salvation and eternal happiness, was bloody on the Cross and today is prolonged in a bloodless manner in every Mass. If every good is derived from the sacrifice of the Cross, indeed, the greatest of goods — the Holy Spirit — then the Holy Mass is also the center and source of energy for all life and for all our educational system. Every family ought to be ordered to the Holy Sacrifice: a day without Mass is a day without the sun! We know that all graces have their primary source in the mercy of the Most Holy Trinity and their source of merits in the sacrifice of the Cross. The Sign of the Cross reminds us of this truth in a very simple way. For this reason, we do well to make the

---

[18]   Thomas Aquinas, *Commentary on the Gospel According to John* C6, L7, no. 974–976, https://aquinas.cc/la/en/~Ioan.C6.L7.

[19]   The substance of this remark is found all throughout Aquinas's treatise on the sacraments. See, for example, *Summa Theologica*, part III, Q. 62, a. 5 and Q. 64, a. 3.

Sign of the Cross conscientiously when we pray together in the family throughout the day, applying our intelligence to meditate on the Passover of Jesus and our affections to give Him thanks for all the gifts that God gives us, first and foremost, the gift of Himself in the various sacraments.

#27

So, were participating in daily Mass and adoring the Eucharist ways in which Carlo translated into actions what he believed?

OF COURSE. AND HE was very faithful to daily Mass and eucharistic adoration. Always, even on vacation. In fact, when we were on vacation in Assisi, he spent even more time before the tabernacle and frequently sought out churches where he knew the Eucharist would be exposed for adoration. Knowing that in the Basilica of Santa Maria degli Angeli every afternoon one could adore the Lord, Carlo always went there. He prayed in silence, recollected in intimate, personal conversation with his Lord. And he would tell us candidly, "The Lord looks at me. And I look at Him. This gazing enriches me. I let the Lord observe me, dig into me, that He might form my soul, that He might shape me. He is truly present; it is not an invention. He is there. If everyone could only realize this, they would run to Him. If everyone would believe in this truth, how it would change their lives."

Carlo copied down this phrase from St. Augustine, "Since no one eats this flesh without first worshipping … we should sin if we did not."[20] This teaches us the best disposition for receiving the Eucharist.

"From the Most Holy Sacrament present in the tabernacle," Carlo would say, "irradiates the healing love that only God knows how to produce, and we unite with the Church triumphant in paradise that is at that moment gathered prostrate before the Lamb of God, to implore grace and blessing for the entire Church. Jesus is present in the tabernacle in that attitude of adoration of the Father, and He wants to draw all men into the same attitude. Jesus wants to teach us to adore the Father as well. In the presence of the Eucharist, we, too, ought to have this attitude of reverence."

He also asked his friends and classmates to adore Jesus in the Eucharist: "Join me," he would say, "and you'll see the revolution that it will bring about within you." We are convinced that from visiting Jesus in the Eucharist in this way, Carlo's charity toward the little ones, the least, and the poor was born.

"The tabernacle is the birthplace of grace," Carlo liked to say.

> In the tabernacle, the Most Holy Trinity is at work. I see the tabernacle as something dynamic. The eucharistic reality is the proof, confirmation, and verification of being destined to holiness. Holiness that is attained through fidelity to the Eucharist and the heroic practice of the seven virtues: the three theological virtues (faith, hope, and charity), and the four cardinal or moral virtues (prudence, justice, fortitude, and temperance). God is our model. Our tools are reason and grace. And grace is given over and over through the sacraments. The tabernacle is near the Holy One, intimately close to the Holy One for twenty centuries now, and

---

20 Augustine, *Exposition on the Psalms* 98, in *The Works of Saint Augustine, a Translation for the 21st Century*, ed. John E. Rotelle, trans. Maria Boulding (New City Press, 2001), 18:474–475.

has become holy. So, frequenting the tabernacle means applying for holiness. But there is also the possibility of non-response, lack of fidelity, hypocrisy, a selfish attitude—and this leads down a risky dead-end road; it is a dangerous one-way ticket.

We go just as we are before the Eucharist, in humility and simplicity. Humility that does not bother to mince words. Simplicity that does not complicate the relationship. We present ourselves such as we are and begin a conversation characterized by familiarity and trust. The visit must be characterized by adoration. Adore. We have to recognize being in the presence of the One God. The distance is infinite, even though the tabernacle is only a few yards away. Adore means bestowing the reverence reserved to God alone, using words fitting to a dialogue with an Absolute Interlocutor, reflecting in one's own interior disposition that one kneels before the Eucharist. The visit is carried out in respectful ways of worship interwoven with faith in the one God, hope in the one God, and love for the one God. Adoration also means climbing the heights of the commandments on Sinai, respecting the precepts of the Church, and walking the paths of the duties of one's own state of life. Other suitable prayers are the Our Father, the Hail Mary, the Glory Be, the prayer to our Guardian Angel, and the prayer for the dead. At the end of a visit to the Eucharist, we place before the Lord our plan for the day, declaring that all will be done for the greater glory of God. The farewell greeting can be expressed by using an ejaculatory prayer such as: "O Jesus, may I love you ever more!" "Lord, take me as I am and make me into what you will!" "I will try to offend you less!" "Lord, I abandon myself into your hands."

We have to enter the mentality of the tabernacle. It's a very special mentality. Baptism is spiritual regeneration. Confirmation is spiritual growth. The Eucharist is spiritual nourishment. The sacrament of the Eucharist, although it has a certain duality at the material level, is *one* in its form and perfection. The Eucharist is the sacrament of unity. Although there are two elements — the bread and the wine that constitute the sacrament of the Eucharist in its entirety, as the Church teaches us — we profess that the sacrament is one only. Baptism is necessary to begin supernatural life. The Eucharist is necessary to bring supernatural life to fulfillment.

The sacrament of the Eucharist has three meanings: the first concerns the past insofar as it commemorates the Passion of the Lord, ritualizing it for us, rendering it present in a bloodless way in every Mass and rendering those who participate in the Mass present to the effects of that sacrifice. For this reason, it is called a *sacrifice*. The second concerns the unity of the Church. For this reason, it is called communion or *synaxis*. The third concerns the future: it is a prefiguration of eternal beatitude and for this reason is called *viaticum*.

There are also three ways of considering the sacrament of the Eucharist: *sacramentum tantum*, the bread and the wine; *res et sacramentum*, the true Body of Christ; and *res tantum*, namely the effect of this sacrament.[21] The Paschal Lamb is the main figure of the Eucharist. Christ instituted this sacrament under the species of bread and wine, ordinary food for rational beings. In this sacrament they are taken separately, the bread as the sacrament of the Body, and the wine as the sacrament of the Blood. This sacrament is the memorial of the Passion of the Lord, that occurs with the separation of the Blood from the Body. The Body of Christ for the salvation of the body. The Blood of Christ for the salvation of the soul.

Beware of emptying the sense of *with you*! We need to prove by our words and actions that the Eucharist exists. It's

---

[21] Here Carlo is making reference to a distinction made by Thomas Aquinas, *Summa Theologica* III. q. 73, a. 6.

enough to turn the corner, open the door, and enter any church... There are people kneeling. A celebration is underway. Something is going on; Someone is present. People will ask and want to know what is going on [to draw all these people]. This is the documented proof; it is the witness's proof; it is the nearly palpable proof of the influence of the Eucharist.

The Eucharist has the sacred right of recognition. It must be spoken of. This reality must be noticed. It must! We're talking about five continents: Europe, Asia, Africa, America, and Oceania. The Eucharist undergoes and bears every single event on the planet. We don't think about it; we don't notice or even take it into account, but when there is an earthquake, an eruption, a flood or other such calamities, the tabernacle is laid waste like everything else. When a catastrophic event is reported, the involvement and destruction of tabernacles is never mentioned in the least. His presence shares it all, participates in it all. His Presence. In the tabernacle and from the tabernacle, the substantial, substantiating, substantive divine presence is at work. This must absolutely be taken into account. He has been there for over twenty centuries. He is next to us. Within the tabernacle there is Life. There is Being. There is Eternity. There is Infinity. It is a world apart. It is a new planet. It is a new star. It must be written in geography and history textbooks. The tabernacle must become the home of all, the residence of each, the meeting place for all people, the point of reference, the measuring rod, the yardstick.

We need to adore in a more profound way, a more personal way. We must give thanks for this gift. Give thanks and recognize the benefits. In this way, we know and feel that we are destined for grace. Thanking, thanksgiving, appreciating the gifts of God. The tabernacle is one of the greatest gifts of God. The tabernacle is the setting of thanksgiving. Here Jesus gives thanks. He thanks the Father. He thanks the Holy Spirit. He thanks them for the Church. He thanks them for every single person. He thanks them for me, for you, for him, for her, for them. Effusions of thanksgiving flow out from the tabernacle. But also propitiation. The Passion continues. Forgiveness must be merited. On our behalf, the tabernacle raises its arms to Heaven.

Carlo liked to use various metaphors to describe what happens in us when we adore the Eucharist:

"Standing in the sun, we get tanned. In the presence of the eucharistic Jesus, we become saints."

"When a thin ray of sunlight enters a darkened room, the dust in the air can be seen with the naked eye. In fact, it is precisely the dust particles that lie along the trajectory of the light beam that spread the light in all directions, as happens to the moon, which we can see in the night sky. The same thing happens with our soul. During eucharistic adoration we are struck by the light that the Eucharist unleashes and are thus capable of seeing all the 'dust' that pollutes our soul and hinders us from making progress along the path of holiness, which is normally not visible to the naked eye."

Adoration satisfied his aspiration to be "silent" in order to "listen to the voice of God," to simplify his personal prayer. Carlo would say that "the more prayer is simple the more it will be profound." And to detach himself from superficial things, he liked to reflect that "to draw near to God it is really important to liberate oneself from oneself and from all superficial things."

"The history of tabernacles," he would say, "is the history of salvation that for two millennia, in a bloodless way, is renewed every moment around the globe. The tabernacles have accompanied it. They have followed it. They have marked it. Every tabernacle has its story, its vicissitudes. And not the simplest ones. Every time a tabernacle is installed, it means a church or a chapel has been built. For twenty centuries, from year to year, there has been an admirable proliferation of tabernacles. If one could make a map of lights from continent to continent, millions would be lit.

"The Eucharist must enter this world and mingle with all who live in this world. The world has to be liberated, purified, and humanized through the Eucharist. This is not a strange or incomprehensible thing to talk about. It is a matter of rehumanizing, of recivilizing, of reintegrating the world. The living and life-giving presence of the Eucharist can be of great use in this. We must try to spread the idea of worship, the culture of worship. Otherwise we run the serious risk of allowing our originality, our exclusivity, to be overwhelmed in a cultural morass. Our culture needs to be 'eucharistized.' This might seem like a utopian endeavor. Yes, it is gigantic, but not impossible. If the Eucharist succeeds in entering this world, in advancing and making headway, in investing the world with itself, then: Victory! Fresh air!

"Just a call or a message and we're in contact with the world of industry, small and great alike. The telephone, radio, TV, computer, Internet—all these are in our home 24/7. In the same way, if we have become 'eucharistic' we will take flight. By means of the Internet, we can travel across continents and through creation. The whole world passes before our eyes. If we could but 'eucharistize' ourselves, we could reach the whole world. Will we be able to do this? If so, then a rushing current would take hold of everything, sweeping it along, gathering and uniting and amassing everything. Given that the Eucharist exists, substantially and vitally, it must be conducted into the multimedia current that has such an enormous flow. It is an ocean of news, ideas, words, advice, suggestions, proposals, insinuations, attempts, interferences, and much more. And we are up to our necks in it. We run the risk of being overwhelmed by it. It is an all-devouring vortex. This is perhaps our last chance to place the Eucharist at the apex. It is almost violent, almost presumptuous, to confine the Eucharist the way it is in tabernacles. The Eucharist risks being given a 'life sentence.' We have the Omnipotent closed, locked up, guarded... There, concealed inside a box, we have the Omniscient, Being, the Essential, the One God, the Triune God, Paradise. He is there, 24/7, non-stop, without bail, without rest, without anything. The Infinite within the finite of a box. The Infinite within the finite of a container. The Infinite within the finite of the *within*."

As a catechist, Carlo compared the presence of Jesus in the tabernacle to a very powerful magnet: as soon as you approach the tabernacle, it attracts all those who sincerely look for Him and makes them fall in love with Him.

As regards eucharistic Consecration, which he knew to be a very important moment of the Mass, Carlo said, "During the Consecration, we must ask for graces from God the Father through the merits of His only Son, Jesus Christ, through His Holy Wounds, His Most Precious Blood, and the Tears and the Sorrows of the Blessed Virgin Mary who, being His Mother, can intercede for us more than anyone." At the end of the Consecration, he would pray the following in his heart: "Through the Sacred Heart of Jesus and the Immaculate Heart of Mary, I offer you all my requests and ask you to grant them." And when he received eucharistic Communion, he said: "Jesus, make yourself at home! My house is your house!" He would often repeat, "You go straight to Heaven if you receive the Eucharist every day!"

He lived with great intensity the moment of thanksgiving after Mass. To live it well he made use of the Latin word ARDOR, composed of the initial letters of Adoration, Thanksgiving [*Ringraziamento*], Request [*Domanda*], Offering, Reparation. He put to good use St. Teresa of Avila's teaching: at the moment of Communion, Jesus is pleased to teach us and we must seek to give Him our attention. And also that of St. Maria Maddalena de' Pazzi:

thanksgiving after Communion is the most precious thanksgiving we have in this life and the most opportune moment for negotiating with God and being inflamed by His divine Love.

#28

We have seen the importance Carlo attributed to the Eucharist, saying that the sacraments were six + one (the Eucharist). What did he say about the other six?

DURING MASS ONE SUNDAY, our parish priest in Santa Maria Segreta in Milan had us renew our baptismal promises. Carlo, who must have been around nine years old, was radiant and excited. After Mass he told us, "The time we are given to live on this earth will never be enough to thank Jesus for the gift of our Baptism. Many don't realize what a gift it is to receive it. Many seem to be more interested in the exterior aspects and the gifts that are usually given on such occasions than in the sacrament as such, which gives us back the divine life we lost due to Original Sin." He also told us how fitting it is to correspond to the grace received through Baptism because, "Baptism, besides being the necessary passage to gain access to the other sacraments, is also the gate to Paradise." In his notes, he wrote:

> We must return to the profound significance of Baptism as an instrument of salvation and a vehicle of grace. Baptism erases the guilt inherited by our ancestors Adam and Eve due to what is known as original sin—the sin of disobeying God that has infected and continues to infect all humanity. Baptism does not, however, heal the wounds that this sin has left and that continually incline us to do evil.

Furthermore, this sacrament is also the gate that allows us to enter the others, which are the instruments provided by the Most Holy Trinity to give us grace and allow us to be entirely healed of this wound. Thus, it also becomes the gateway that allows us to obtain salvation.

Carlo also wrote some notes on the Anointing of the Sick:

Anointing of the Sick (and no longer, as it once was called, Extreme Unction). Even if they are unaware of it, most people face the moment of passing away filled with worries of not being sufficiently purified and prepared. This is why there is a sacrament specifically for this great moment. Today it is called the Anointing of the Sick because it is meant for every person who is seriously ill in body or spirit. And for the afflictions of the spirit, it accompanies and follows the sacrament of Confession of sins (therefore, we must not wait until we are at the point of death to receive it!). And there are special prayers. But the faithful have to play their part in preparing themselves to meet death. In other words, life should be a continuous preparation for death. We must not abandon ourselves to the terrifying temptation to despondency and fear, but neither should we be superficial and negligent. A balance is needed, an equilibrium nourished especially by trust and oriented toward the gates of hope. This second of the theological virtues should be our lighthouse and our strength. Scripture admonishes us to "make a defense to anyone who calls you to account for the hope that is in you" (1 Pet. 3:15).

When existence is under attack by illness, or when the definitive death sentence has been given, we must conform ourselves freely to the divine will. Furthermore, it is an excellent exercise to unite ourselves intimately with the Passion and Death of the Lord. Paul said that what was lacking in the Passion of Christ was being made up in him:

this means that the Mystical Body is always climbing Calvary and is here and there subjected to humiliations and persecutions and struggles. Just like Creation, the Passion continues as well, until the end of the world, this world. Uniting ourselves in this way has advantageous repercussions on the entire People of God. In this way, a continuous circuit of suffering and offering and martyrdom is established. This circuit accompanies that of the Mass celebrated five times every second. "Jesus, my Communion!" "Jesus, I unite myself to the Masses of the world." These are two fruitful ejaculatory prayers. Very fruitful! Why not make use of them?

Concerning Confession or Reconciliation, he told Rajesh, who was preparing for Baptism: "God is very pleased when souls frequently receive His great gifts—the Eucharist and the sacrament of Confession."

He frequently went to Confession and prepared himself with a good examination of conscience. "First of all," Carlo would say, "we must examine ourselves, plumb our depths, seeing the condition we are in, deep down. We must put our virtues and vices in the balance, our good qualities and bad qualities. A statistical analysis of merits and demerits. And all this without excuses, without fudging, without concessions. Once we have clarified all this, we must come up with a plan of amendment. For example, a project that might seem obvious at first sight, almost cliché, is to remove one defect per year, and conquer one virtue per year. But we must be sincere and faithful in our examination. Being ready and resolute in our proposals. Furthermore, we must try to renew the supernatural in our interior through prayer, meditation on the Word of God, and the steadfast frequenting of the sacraments, in particular Communion and Confession, united with good spiritual direction."

Carlo considered the sacraments in close relation to the Incarnation of the Word. The Word, the second Person of the Most Holy Trinity, became flesh. He assumed our human nature. His person was not a human person but a Divine Person. (The union of human nature with the divine nature is called hypostatic union, namely, divine and human nature in one Divine Person). Why did Christ do this? To redeem humanity that had fallen into sin. The Word suffers in His human nature and in His Divine Person merits. Thus we are saved. Grace has returned. We have been re-adopted as sons. We have been re-destined to co-eternity. This is our destiny. Existence has been reordered in this precise sense. Therefore, from Baptism to Confirmation to Communion, in Reconciliation, Matrimony, Sacred Orders, and the Anointing of the Sick, we receive grace and in this way are led into co-eternity. "The Word became flesh" (John 1:14). God was incarnated and all the phases of His life, from the Incarnation to the Ascension, are for our salvation, to bestow grace upon us. This must be preserved. Preserved in the sacraments. Increased through eucharistic Communion—daily, one would hope—and lived generously throughout the day with works of mercy.

#29

Many of the people who spent time with Carlo remember his contagious, enthusiastic faith.

AS A CHILD, AND later as an adolescent, Carlo was enthusiastic about life and his personal relationship with Jesus. He was also very simple and spontaneous. These are perhaps the most decisive traits of his ability to be contagious. We see this in the accounts of some of the people who lived with him.

The first is Elisa, a young teacher who accompanied him in the afternoon. In 1995, Carlo's maternal grandfather died suddenly. Antonia, being an only child, then had to work with her mother Luana in some of the family businesses and asked Elisa to help Carlo in the afternoon. Beata had already got Carlo into the habit of going to Mass every day. So, even during those months, Carlo wanted to go to Mass and asked Elisa to accompany him. And so she did. Thanks to Carlo's insistence, Elisa returned to living her faith. This teacher recalls how Carlo's insistence was not in the least infantile or capricious. On the contrary, Elisa was always impressed by the spiritual maturity of the child, by his ability to console her pain, and by his composure in prayer.

The second concerns Rajesh, our domestic worker in Milan. Rajesh came from a Hindu family of Brahmins. Carlo often spoke to him about Jesus, the gospel, miracles, and the sacraments. He invited him to recite some prayers together. In the end, he led him to love Jesus such that Rajesh wanted to receive Baptism, and then Confirmation and eucharistic Communion. Once he became a Christian, he would pray regularly with Carlo and at times they prayed the Rosary together. For Carlo, he was not only a point of reference, but also, as he would call him, "my trusty friend Rajesh." They played together, and Rajesh had fun being a clown or an actor in a spy role, and often Carlo would record him with his video camera. During the canonical process introduced by the Archdiocese of Milan, Rajesh remembered Carlo in his testimony (p. 170–171) as follows:

> Given Carlo's profound religiosity and the great faith he had, it was normal that he would often give me catechism lessons on the Catholic religion, me being a Hindu of the

Brahmin priestly caste. Carlo said that one day I would be happier if I drew near to Jesus and he often instructed me using the Bible, the *Catechism of the Catholic Church* and the stories of the saints. Carlo knew the *Catechism* almost by heart and he explained it in such a brilliant way that he was able to get me excited about the importance of the sacraments. He was very gifted at teaching theological concepts that not even adults were able to explain. Little by little I started to take Carlo's advice and instructions seriously, until I eventually decided to be baptized a Christian.

For me, Carlo was a master of authentically lived Christian life and an example of exceptional morality. I wanted to be baptized because Carlo inspired me and struck me with his profound faith, his great charity and purity, which I always considered beyond the norm because such a young, handsome, and wealthy boy would normally prefer to lead a very different life. Carlo was such an example of lofty spirituality and sanctity that I felt within myself the desire to become a Christian and to be able to receive Communion. He had explained to me the importance of receiving the Eucharist daily and of praying to the Virgin Mary using the Holy Rosary, seeking to imitate her heroic virtues. The child always told me that virtues are acquired mainly through an intense sacramental life and that the Eucharist is certainly the apex of charity and that through this sacrament the Lord makes us complete persons, made in His image, and he quoted to me the words that he knew by heart from chapter six of the Gospel according to the apostle John, where Jesus says, "He who eats my flesh and drinks my blood abides in me and I in him and I will raise him up on the last day" (cf. John 6:54, 56); and afterward he explained to me that the Eucharist is the Heart of Christ.

Once, he also told me of the importance of the practice of the devotion of the First Fridays of the Month to the

Sacred Heart of Jesus and the First Five Saturdays of the Month to the Immaculate Heart of Mary. He said that "the Heart of Jesus and the Heart of Mary are indissolubly united" and that when we receive Communion we are in direct contact with Our Lady and the saints in Heaven. "God is very pleased when souls frequently receive His great gifts—the Eucharist and the sacrament of Confession." He also explained to me and prepared me to receive the sacrament of Confirmation, telling me how important it was. He told me how, when he received the sacrament of Confirmation, he had felt within himself a mysterious power that surrounded him and that since that moment his devotion to the Eucharist has grown. When I received the sacrament of Confirmation I felt the same thing.

What struck me most about Carlo was his great purity and his fidelity to daily Mass. Carlo had such a luminous vision of the Catholic Faith that he could infect anyone with the serenity and sweetness by which he presented the truths of Faith.

But the main contagion spread to us in the family. Grandma Luana comes to mind. Here are her words during the process of the Archdiocese of Milan: "Neither I nor his parents were very devout before Carlo led us to the Faith. He was the one who led us to God, to faith, to the joy of knowing how beautiful it is to believe in God.... For almost my entire life, though I had spent ten years in a religious boarding school, I was definitely not a good Catholic. Thanks to Carlo, who from a very young age asked me to go to Mass with him and his mother, I found the faith that I had lost."[22]

His curiosity, his questions about Jesus, about the saints, and about the sacraments, led us to deepen our faith through study. His

---

[22] *Positio super vita, virtutibus*, 276, 279, quoted in C. Acutis and G. M. Carbone, *Originali o fotocopie?* (Bologna: Itinerari Della Fede, 2021), 36.

fidelity to daily Mass, adoration, and personal prayer, his constant desire to imitate Jesus and to practice fraternal charity with everyone, helped us to live the Faith in a more substantial and authentic manner. His example encouraged us to go to the heart of our faith and of fraternal charity and to detach ourselves from what is superficial.

For example, we were very struck by the fact that he was so generous with others, while always being very sober in what concerned himself. We had a hard time buying clothes for him. He said he didn't need anything. When, at the beginning of the school year, I wanted to give him new shoes, he always refused. He wanted only one pair of shoes, and until they were completely worn out, he would continue to use them. With the money saved in this way, he wanted us to help some needy people he knew. Even his classmates or neighborhood friends knew that Carlo was not into following the latest fashion but was quite sober in the clothes he wore and always sought to keep a low profile.

Then, if Carlo knew of people who were far from God, he would immediately start praying for them. "If Providence has put them next to me," he would say, "it's so that I can offer prayers of intercession for them." And in this way, offering the recitation of the Rosary, praying to the Madonna of Pompei, offering Masses with these specific intentions, he obtained many graces of physical healing and conversion. For example, he met a lady who was an invalid and very far from the Faith. She told him that she had not been to Mass in over forty years. Carlo began to pray for her and to have other people pray for her. After a short while, this woman not only was healed of her physical affliction but converted, went to Confession, and started going to Mass again. In fact, she started going every day, just like Carlo.

Today we would say that Carlo was an *influencer* of God, an authentic and efficacious one. Certainly not an influencer of the world, ignorant of his own Creator and Savior, or worse, rejecting Him. Just open the newspapers, turn on the TV, or scroll social media and see how surrounded we are by highly dubious celebrities, who are often created ad hoc by the media or by agencies that manipulate public opinion and then exalted and pumped up. Think of the actors, singers, sports stars, and influencers of various types, who propose ideals destined for the dustbin, despite all their glitter. They seem to be authentic goods but are false, or at best are simply transitory goods that have no relationship with the lasting goods of faith and charity. Carlo placed his bets on the latter.

Or think of the gurus, life coaches, magicians, astrologers, and motivators to whom so many people turn to escape their insecurities, resolve their anxieties, or find light at the end of the tunnel. Carlo found security, happiness, and light in Jesus. And he did so with the enthusiasm and simplicity of a boy who accompanied many others in making this same discovery.

And we, his parents, count ourselves among them.

#30

Antonia and Andrea, you acknowledge having been infected. But surely you have given as well. The path of faith in Christ is never a solitary one; it is trod together. As parents, you, too, have participated. How?

PERHAPS THE MOST SUITABLE image for this path we have walked together is the process of osmosis: we have simultaneously received and given. It all happened in such a smooth manner, without forcing the matter, but with enthusiasm, joy, and simplicity, through his love for us.

Looking back, we recognize an element that helped us to grow together: pilgrimages. We did many of them. We'll recall just a few.

For example, the one we took to Paris, an elegant city, full of museums that we visited attentively, but also a city full of witnesses to the Faith. In Rue du Bac we visited the chapel of the Sisters of Charity where [the incorrupt heart of] their founder, St. Vincent de Paul, and also [the incorrupt body of] St. Catherine Labouré can be venerated. She was the nun to whom Our Lady appeared in 1830, showing Catherine the so-called Miraculous Medal. On the front it is written, "O Mary conceived without sin, pray for us who have recourse to Thee." And on the back, the upper part features a cross above an M standing for Mary; on the lower part are two hearts, one crowned with thorns, the Sacred Heart of Jesus, and the other pierced with a sword, the Immaculate Heart of Mary. Catherine also heard these words, *"Have a medal made according to this model. For those who wear it with confidence, there will be abundant graces."*[23] Aware of these facts, Carlo commented, "With this medal the Lord wanted to emphasize the special role that His Mother Mary plays in the economy of humanity's salvation. Besides being the mediatrix of all graces, perhaps the Lord wanted to tell us that Mary is also the co-redemptrix of all humanity: that on the medal the M of Mary overlaps the I of *Iesus*, topped by the Cross, signifying that the Blessed Virgin is associated with Jesus' sacrifice of redemption."

In Rue des Archives, we visited the church where a eucharistic miracle occurred at Easter of 1290. A nonbeliever who hated the Catholic Faith and did not believe in the Real Presence of Christ in the Eucharist had gotten ahold of a consecrated Host and profaned it: he struck it repeatedly with a knife and then tossed it into boiling

---

[23] "The Apparitions and the Miraculous Medal," Chapelle Notre Dame de la Medaille Miraculeuse, https://www.chapellenotredamedelamedaillemirac uleuse.com/langues/english/apparitions-et-la-medaille-miraculeuse-gb/.

water. But the Host arose out of the water to the stunned amazement of the profaner, who then hastened to restore the Host to a pious woman who immediately handed it over to her parish priest. The news of this prodigious event spread immediately throughout Paris, to the point that the bishop, the king, and the people decided to transform the house of the profaner into a chapel in which the Sacred Host is preserved.

Another trip/pilgrimage was to Spain in 2005. We had already enrolled Carlo at the Leone XIII High School in Milan, founded by the Jesuits. So, we thought we would visit Manresa, in Catalonia, where Ignatius of Loyola lived for eleven years and had his conversion from being a noble knight with a fiery temperament to becoming a passionate friend of the Lord. It was also at Manresa that he wrote the *Spiritual Exercises* so that others might experience the liberation and salvation of the encounter with the Lord Jesus. We went on to the Marian shrine of Montserrat, run by Benedictine monks, where on March 24, 1522, Ignatius abandoned the sword and dagger on Our Lady's altar and put on the pilgrim's cloak as a sign of his new life as a disciple of Jesus. Then we reached Barcelona. Carlo was enchanted by the visit to the Sagrada Família, the basilica constructed by the architect Antoni Gaudí. He wrote in his travel diary,

> True originality consists in returning to the origin, which is God. Creation continues incessantly through man's mediation. Man does not create but discovers and then sets off from this discovery. Those who probe the laws of nature so as to create new works, collaborate with the Creator; those who merely copy, do not collaborate. For this reason, originality consists in returning to the origin.

Before beginning these pilgrimages/trips we would read something about the places we wanted to visit. We had read something about the life and major work of architect Antoni Gaudí. According to the official Act of the laying of the first stone on March 19, 1882, the Basilica of the Sagrada Família was constructed explicitly to "awaken from their torpor hearts that have fallen asleep, exalt the Faith and give warmth to charity." Carlo immediately had a great veneration of Gaudí; and, knowing that the process for his canonization was underway, he began to turn to him in prayer that he, too, might glorify Jesus, who makes Himself truly present in the Eucharist, becoming our food and drink.

An obligatory stop was made in Lourdes. When Carlo reached the grotto of Massabielle, he renewed his vow to Mary to be always faithful to the daily recitation of the Rosary and then consecrated himself to the Immaculate Heart. After drinking the water from the grotto, he stayed there for over an hour in prayer. We visited the Moulin de Boly, the miserable house where Bernadette was born. Reading Bernadette's story and that of the apparitions of Our Lady, we found among the messages that Mary gave to Bernadette the promise that she would not make her happy in this world, but rather in the next; the invitation to offer personal sacrifices, saying three times, "Penance! Penance! Penance!"; and the recommendation to recite and have others recite the Holy Rosary. Carlo welcomed Mary's invitation to prayer, penance, and sacrifice for others.

Upon returning to Italy, Carlo told his friends about the significance of the apparitions of 1858 and how he had been struck by Bernadette's experience, this illiterate adolescent, the poor daughter of the common people, chosen by God and by Our Lady for her simplicity and humility. During the apparition of March 25, 1858, Mary revealed to Bernadette that she was the Immaculate Conception. Bernadette was completely ignorant of the meaning of this title, nor did she know that four years earlier Pope Pius IX had proclaimed the dogma of the Immaculate Conception. Carlo wrote the following in his notes:

Mother of God. Creature risen to Infinity. Giving herself to God, abandoning herself to God, she finds herself the Mother of God. Now we have one of our own elevated, sublimated, "celestialized." Mother of God: three words, four syllables, eleven letters, a poem. The entire universe was in some way involved. At least Heaven, the Angels, the Archangels, the Thrones, the Dominions, the Virtues, the Powers, the Principalities, the Cherubims, the Seraphim must have perceived the event. We are the superficial ones, the ignorant ones. We ought to feel part of this beatifying situation. She who was preserved from Original Sin, overshadowed by the Father, rendered a mother through the power of the Holy Spirit, is one of us. We must not pronounce the words *Holy Mother of God* habitually or familiarly or superficially. We have to consider them theologically, spiritually. *Mother of God*: Being with being. The Infinite with the finite. The Eternal with time. The Creator with the creature.

Every year, from August to September, when we were guests at Carlo's paternal grandparents' in Santa Margherita Ligure, we would always go on pilgrimage to a nearby shrine dedicated to the Madonna of Montallegro. In 1597, Mary appeared there to Giovanni Chichizola, introducing herself as the Mother of God, asking him to build a church on the site, and then showing him a spring of water considered to be miraculous. We made this little pilgrimage in 2006 as well. Carlo confided to us that he had asked Mary in prayer to be able to go straight to Paradise without passing through Purgatory. When the stairs leading to the sanctuary filled with pilgrims—some of them severely handicapped—Carlo quickly dashed to help them. We had brought some empty bottles and went to the spring to fill them with water. Carlo said to us, "It's important to take advantage of these gifts of Heaven, because all these free gifts are useful for our progress on our personal spiritual path, in growing and being helped to defeat our defects and weaknesses."

Every year, when we were on vacation in Cilento, we always went to the shrine of the Madonna of Pompei. Carlo was very fond of this place. When he was just four years old, he made the consecration to her on his own initiative. He was also devoted to the founder of the sanctuary, Bl. Bartolo Longo, who went from being a prestigious lawyer on the Naples bar association to being the international promoter of the prayer of the Rosary.

In the summer of 2006, we went to Portugal. Our destination was Fatima. First, we passed through Santarém, also in Portugal, the place where two eucharistic miracles are celebrated. In 1247, a young woman, jealous on account of her husband, consulted a sorceress who told her to steal a consecrated Host and to bring it to her so she could make a love potion. Thus, the woman stole the consecrated Host and wrapped it in her veil. But the veil was soon soaked with blood, so the woman ran home; when she unwrapped the cloth, she saw blood oozing out of the Host. Terrorized and confused, she hid it all in a drawer in their bedroom. From there, powerful rays of light began to come forth. Her husband noticed the phenomenon and notified the parish priest. The latter went into the house, took the Host, and, adoring it, brought it back to the church of St. Stephen's. The Host was encased in a beeswax reliquary and continued to bleed for three days. Many years later, in 1340, there was a second miracle: a priest opened the tabernacle and found the beeswax reliquary shattered and, in its place, a crystal pyx with the miraculous Host and Blood inside.

After our stop in Santarém, we continued on to Fatima. Once we arrived, we were welcomed by a nun who is a friend of ours and by Fr. Luis Kondor, the postulator at that time for the causes of Francisco and Jacinta Marto. As he guided us through a rich photographic exhibit, he told us about many episodes from the 1917 apparitions to the three shepherd children, Jacinta (seven years old), Francisco (nine), and Lucia (ten). During the various apparitions, Our Lady told them, "Pray the Rosary every day, in order to obtain peace for the world, and the end of the war."[24] Lucia, who later became a Carmelite nun, said, "In these last times in which we are living, the Blessed Virgin has given a new efficacy to the praying of the Holy Rosary ... in such a way that there is no problem that cannot be resolved by praying the Rosary, no matter how difficult it is ... in the spiritual life of each of us or the lives of our families ... or even in the lives of peoples and nations."[25]

Carlo said, "From beginning to end, Our Lady reveals to us in a meaningful way in Fatima the love that the Most Holy Trinity has for us and the mercy that God gives through the Immaculate Heart of Mary."

In Fatima, everything urged us to make a concrete, direct experience of God. Carlo was struck that in the apparition on May 13, 1917, Our Lady had proposed to the shepherds, "Are you willing to offer yourselves to God and bear all the sufferings He wills to send you, as an act of reparation for the sins by which He is offended, and of supplication for the conversion of sinners?" Responding on behalf of all, Lucia replied, "Yes, we are willing." According to Lucia's testimony, Mary then "opened her hands for the first time, communicating to us a light so intense that, as it streamed from her hands, its rays penetrated our hearts and the innermost depths of our souls, making us see ourselves in God, Who was that light, more clearly than we see

---

[24] Sr. Lucia, *Fatima in Lucia's Own Words*, 176.

[25] Sr. Lucia of Fatima, interview by Fr. Augustin Fuentes, December 26, 1957, as recorded in Joaquín María Alonso, *La verdad sobre el Secreto de Fátima, Fátima sin mitos* (Centro Mariano, 1976), https://www.traditio ninaction.org/HotTopics/g23ht_Interview.html.

ourselves in the best of mirrors. Then, moved by an interior impulse that was also communicated to us, we fell on our knees, repeating in our hearts: *O most Holy Trinity, I adore You! My God, my God, I love You in the most Blessed Sacrament!*"[26] Mary's proposal to the three children echoed what Jesus taught through His words, "If any man would come after me, let him deny himself and take up his cross daily and follow me. For whoever would save his life will lose it; and whoever loses his life for my sake, he will save it. For what does it profit a man if he gains the whole world and loses or forfeits himself?" (Luke 9:23–25).

Carlo was fascinated by the mystical aspect of the apparitions and teachings of Fatima. For example, Carlo noticed that the prayer that was taught to the three visionaries, *My God, I believe, adore, hope, and love You. I ask your forgiveness for all those who do not believe, do not adore, do not hope, and do not love You,* refers explicitly to the three theological virtues, faith, hope, and charity, the pillars of the sacrament of Baptism. In Fatima, God is placed in the center, and man receives the explicit invitation to adore Him and love Him. And the message of Fatima is a message of hope, because Mary says in the final apparition, "In the end, my Immaculate Heart shall triumph."[27] Our Lady announced to Lucia that Jacinta and Francisco would soon be in Paradise, whereas she, Lucia, would continue to live on this earth to foster devotion to her Immaculate Heart. In her memoirs, Lucia recalled repeatedly the great promise of Our Lady that filled her with joy: "I will never forsake you. My Immaculate Heart will be your refuge and the way that will lead you to God."[28]

Carlo made his personal consecration to the Immaculate Heart of Mary on several occasions in a solemn way, in church during a

---

[26] Sr. Lucia, *Fatima in Lucia's Own Words*, 175–176.
[27] Ibid. 105, 162.
[28] Ibid. 67, 107, 126, 161, 195.

communal celebration for this purpose. And he renewed it every day with these words, "Immaculate Heart of Mary, I consecrate myself totally to you forever, with all those dear to me."

We could go on and on with such memories. We will limit ourselves to shedding light on just some of the aspects that were decisive to our growth in faith. We organized those pilgrimages/road trips by reading the story of the place and of the people who had contributed to its development. Then, along the route, we would pray together in the car. Once we arrived, we would go to Confession, participate in Mass, and formulate specific life proposals. Then, we would go through what we could remember of the stories that we had read trying to find the places described. And when possible, we also tried to encounter people who could give testimony to the events linked to the shrine, such as the miracles that had occurred there. That was what happened, for example, in Fatima. Carlo often took a lot of photos and made videos with his camera and collected documentary material for the exhibits he would put together. They were moments of great spiritual communion that edified us all. For example, we will never forget the long lines of candles on the sides of the grotto of Lourdes. At sunset, they illuminated the banks of the Gave. The light they radiated spoke of the hope, the suffering and anguish, and the faith of so many people. And we, too, lit our candles together.

#31

Can you remember some of Carlo's personality traits that contributed to making his faith so contagious?

THE FIRST ONE THAT comes to mind was his optimism. He was always positive, with a lively sense of humor. He would always tell us, "Sadness is turning one's gaze toward oneself; happiness is turning one's gaze toward God." In fact, we never saw him sad, not even when he was admitted to the hospital in October 2006.

In general, as a child and then adolescent, he never complained. And that's how he remained, even during his last days in the hospital. The medical staff in the two clinics where he was treated was amazed by his serenity and smile in confronting his illness and severe discomfort. Even in those moments, he would say, "Not me, but God." And then, "Not self-love, but the glory of God." In the days before that, when he only had a fever, he told us, "I offer my sufferings for the pope, for the Church, to avoid Purgatory and go straight to Heaven." Being always cheerful and witty, we thought he was joking. In reality, these were all expressions of his faith: his intelligence was rooted in the mystery of Jesus' life, whom he knew was the Lord, the Savior, the Friend who gave His life for His disciples. And this gave him great inner strength, an ability to see beyond the suffering or the troubles of the moment, and so the ability to be detached—which is essential to having a sense of humor.

These were the results of a life, however brief, lived in the habit of soothing the most difficult situations, in bolstering the spirits of those who were sad and dejected, in consoling those going through difficult moments of affliction and mourning. He never succumbed to resignation or, worse, to desperation, because he had abandoned himself to Jesus.

Fr. Roberto Gazzaniga, the Jesuit priest who was the principal of Leone XIII High School in Milan, collected some of the testimonies and memories of Carlo's classmates: "The character traits that most struck them and that remained etched in the memories and lives of the kids are his joy, vivacity, generosity, desire to befriend, capacity for self-discipline—*I never saw him get angry, even when provoked*—his commitment to various interests without ever neglecting his duties; he was smiling, kind, on good terms with everyone—*If you were in a bad mood, being near him you'd get over it;* then there was his contagious optimism, his capacity for socio-political interests *in a phase of growth when attention to oneself and one's own little world often prevails, sympathetic with a welcoming style even in the sense of taking the initiative and welcoming friends into his home, feeling that with him words did not fall into polite listening, but that there was a real interest in the person.* In particular, Carlo's spontaneity, availability, and affability struck his classmates a lot."

#32

Another of Carlo's expressions was: "Every minute that passes is one minute fewer that we have to sanctify ourselves."

THE EXPRESSION "ONE MINUTE fewer" might make some people anxious. For Carlo, it was a stimulus to giving his best, without anxiety, but with spontaneity and constancy, living virtuously for love, caring for his soul and his spiritual life. "Why are people so concerned about their bodies but are not concerned about the beauty of their souls?

The beauty of the body is like that of a rose, it lasts for a short while but is destined to wilt immediately." He also compared exterior beauty to a sandcastle built on the beach: as soon as the first wave reaches it, it is destroyed, and you're left with a mound of sand. Whereas spiritual beauty remains forever. It consists of virtuous actions, works of faith, hope, and above all charity toward God and mercy toward our neighbor.

Carlo also said, "All our efforts at staying forever aesthetically young and beautiful are totally useless. It will all fade anyway. What will render us truly beautiful in God's eyes is only the way in which we have loved Him and how we have loved our brothers."

Carlo had the intuition of taking care of his spiritual beauty. We think this came about because the Holy Spirit inspired him, because he had been counseled well by some priests and by good examples, by his nanny Beata in particular. He knew how to cultivate the virtues, as the great spiritual author Evagrius Ponticus (d. 399) taught. This Church Father left us precious advice, formulated as phrases or aphorisms on life, to form our spiritual life properly. In his *Treatise on the Practical Life* he writes,

> When the mind wanders, reading, vigils, and prayer bring it to a standstill. When desire bursts into flame, hunger, toil, and anachoresis [solitude] extinguish it. When the irascible part becomes agitated, psalmody, patience, and mercy calm it. But these practices are to be engaged in at the appropriate times and in due measure, for what is done without due measure or not at the opportune moment lasts but a little while; and what is short-lived is more harmful than it is profitable. [29]

[29] Evagrius of Pontus, *Praktikos* 15, in *Evagrius of Pontus: The Greek Ascetical Corpus,* trans. Robert E. Sinkewicz (Oxford: Oxford University Press, 2003).

Those who knew Carlo recognized that he was always cheerful, an exterior sign of the fact that he was victorious in governing his emotions or passions. Again, Evagrius teaches that "the passions are naturally set in motion by the senses. When love and abstinence are present, they will not be set in motion; when [these virtues] are absent, [the passions] will be set in motion."[30] Once our virtues govern the world of the passions and emotions, there will arise "humility and compunction, tears, an infinite longing for the divine and an immeasurable zeal for work."[31]

In his counsels, we also find this original and amusing piece of advice: "When you experience temptation, do not pray before you have directed some words of anger against the one causing the affliction [the devil]. For when your soul is affected by thoughts, it follows that your prayer is not pure. But if you speak some angry word against them, you confound and dispel the mental representations coming from your adversaries. This is the natural function of anger, even in the case of good mental representations."[32]

[30]   Ibid. 38.
[31]   Ibid. 57.
[32]   Ibid. 42.

#33

You have told of the importance that Carlo attributed to the virtuous life and in particular to charity through adoration, the Mass, and fraternal solicitude. Can you tell us something about Carlo's other human virtues in daily life?

HE NEVER COMPARED HIMSELF with others, not because he considered himself better than others like an arrogant person, but because he was simple, modest, and preferred to keep a low profile, not wanting in any way to make a show of himself. He once told us, "Why diminish the light of others to make your own shine brighter?" This expression revealed how far he was from jealousy. In his first year in high school, he received a 9 out of 10 on an essay. That day he had the highest grade in the class. Two of his classmates, considered to be the brightest of the class, got much lower grades and cried because Carlo had gotten a 9. Carlo, amazed by their reactions, told us he had tried to console the two classmates by telling them that he did not deserve the 9 and that the teacher had been too lenient with him.

He did not grumble, nor did he criticize others, and he certainly did not appreciate those who criticized others. He tried in every way not to take part in these destructive conversations. He was opposed to all that: he helped his classmates to be successful in their studies, in sports, and in their spiritual life, and rejoiced and congratulated them when they succeeded.

One of the qualities that his friends most appreciated in Carlo was his loyalty and veracity. If he gave his word, he stood by it. He knew nothing about lying. When he taught catechism, he told of the episode narrated by a spiritual daughter of Padre Pio of Pietrelcina: "We all know that Padre Pio did not want anyone to tell a lie, not even jokingly or for something of little importance. To keep the commitment I had made in the confessional, I began to ask for help from my Guardian Angel. When I found myself in difficulty, because they asked me something I didn't know and I couldn't respond without falling into a lie, I commended myself to him." [33]

He had a great capacity for self-control in all senses, not only regarding temperance, but also in his speech and the use of time. For example, as a little boy, in order not to disturb us adults or interrupt our work, he was able to play alone for hours, to read, or to draw cartoons. Tantrums were foreign to him. Elisa, the teacher who was with him some afternoons, was struck by his self-control in using his time well between studies and play, prayer and time with friends.

He was temperate even in eating. If there was a dish that he did not like, he would eat it anyhow. When there were sweets or other tasty dishes, he knew how to wait until everyone else was served, and then if there was something left over, he would take some, too. He admitted openly that he had a sweet tooth, and he always ate with a hearty appetite. But he never ate between meals. In the summer of 1999, we went overboard on pizza and gelato and we were all a bit overweight. When we returned to Milan, he immediately began to be more moderate with food and slimmed down. For Carlo, moderation with food was not merely a matter of diet or eating healthily, but also the possibility of offering to God some little sacrifice, a little renunciation of something licit and good in view of doing something better. For example, he offered the little sacrifice of a snack or some sweet to help the souls of the departed in Purgatory. Sometimes he even renounced watching a film that he liked, over and above

---

[33] "Le figlie spirituali di Padre Pio: così ci ha soccorso l'angelo custode," August 16, 2020, *Aleteia*, https://www.sanfrancescopatronoditalia.it/notizie/fede/le-figlie-spirituali-di-padre-pio-cos%C3%AC-ci-ha-soccorso-l%E2%80%99angelo-custode-49222.

avoiding violent or vulgar ones. When he was little, he preferred cartoons or documentaries about animals. As he grew, he preferred action films, or documentaries on the events of the Bible and the lives of the saints.

Several months after his death, the commission of the Archdiocese of Milan in charge of his beatification process examined the chronology of his activities on his personal computer. The last activity dated from the day before he was admitted to the hospital. The commission discovered that the websites Carlo visited concerned his high school subjects, information technology, and above all, subjects relating to faith. There were no websites related to pornography. This offers further proof of the good use he made of his time, of his temperance, and also of his chastity.

As a catechist and companion, Carlo proposed to his friends the same rectitude and purity that he was living thanks to his faith. On various occasions, we heard Carlo insisting with his friends on living a chaste life and not wasting their time on pornography and sins of impurity. He often told them, "The tempter puts us to the test in this matter where we might be weak. We must not be afraid, but only flee from him with resolve. Without the consent of our will, the tempter can do nothing against us. Through pornography and sins of impurity, the devil takes so many souls to Hell." And he quoted the words of Mary in Fatima, "Sins that bring most souls to Hell are the sins of the flesh."[34] He was not afraid of repeating to his friends what the *Catechism* teaches: "Pornography ... does grave injury to the dignity of its participants (actors, vendors, the public), since each one becomes an object of base pleasure and illicit profit for others. It

---

[34]   This affirmation is recorded in the conversation of Jacinta with Mother Superior Maria da Purificagao Godinho, in John de Marchi, *The True Story of Fatima: A Complete Account of the Fatima Apparitions* (Fatima Center, 2009), 70.

immerses all who are involved in the illusion of a fantasy world. It is a grave offense. Civil authorities should prevent the production and distribution of pornographic materials" (2354).

His chastity transpired from his gaze as well, and in the attention he dedicated to others. "It is important always to keep watch over ourselves," Carlo would say. "Only by maintaining our purity of heart will we be able to accumulate in Heaven the treasure needed for Eternity." He knew that purity of heart, of the affections, and of the eyes goes hand in hand with moderating the daily aspects of life, like our way of dressing and walking. He knew that sensuality and all its "accessories" must be shunned because they distance us from appreciating the beauty and the image that God has impressed on us—we are the *temple of the Most Holy Trinity*—and because they pollute our way of loving. Finally, he knew that temperance and chastity are gifts of God. Therefore, he always prayed to God that he might keep his baptismal innocence, something we must all guard jealously. He asked God and his Guardian Angel with great confidence to be aided in living always in sanctifying grace.

Other human virtues we remember in Carlo are his constancy, his loyalty, and his fortitude in sports. He certainly had the good fortune of playing many sports from the time he was five: mini-soccer, skiing, swimming, karate, kung-fu, tennis, volleyball, and track. At different ages, he was passionately committed to each of these, but without competitiveness or vindictiveness. For Carlo, playing sports was about cultivating friendships most of all, living moments of joy with his friends, growing together toward a goal that was good and motivating, putting his physical abilities to the test, overcoming fears and fatigue, and triumphing over the difficulties within the team. He never asked us to try high-risk sports like parkour or hand gliding.

#34

I'll move on to some uncomfortable questions, and I address Antonia. In the Gospel according to John, it says, "He who believes in the Son has eternal life; he who does not obey the Son shall not see life, but the wrath of God rests upon him" (3:36). The wrath of God is a recurring theme in biblical historical revelation, and yet many prefer to censure it.

THE WRATH OF GOD is a very frequent image in Sacred Scripture (cf. Exod. 15:8, 32:10; Num. 12:9; Ps. 2:5, 12; Rom. 1:18; Eph. 2:3, just to quote a few examples). It is a metaphorical image applied to God: God is pure spirit, without a body, and therefore cannot have passions or emotions as the human soul has. This metaphorical image signifies the punishment awaiting the wicked, namely sinners, and is strictly associated with the saving justice of God (cf. Mic. 7:9; Zeph. 3:1–10; Rom. 5:9; 1 Thess. 1:10). God wills directly and positively the salvation of all, whereas He only indirectly wills punishment, only because punishment is the personal consequence for those who obstinately and knowingly refuse the saving action of Christ.

The opinion has spread among many believers that Hell is empty. But this opinion is refuted by a number of facts.

First of all, when we Italians think of Hell, we are conditioned by Dante's *Divine Comedy* and we imagine it as a place. I think, however, that it should be considered mainly as an eventual life condition: the damned, whether an angel or a human, obstinately rejects God. And yet he stands in God's presence. And God manifests Himself for what He is, namely Merciful Love. The damned knows very well that God is Merciful Love, and yet he is closed in his obstinacy and in his rejection of God. This produces the punishment itself in the damned angel or damned human. It is something quite dramatic and excruciating: the damned know that God exists and that He is limitless Mercy, but they remain closed in hatred and rejection.

In the months before his death, Carlo was preparing photos and captions for a new exhibit titled "Hell, Purgatory, and Paradise." In some of this material, he collected, for example, what Our Lady revealed in Fatima to the three children concerning Hell. On June 13, 1917, the Blessed Virgin Mary exhorted them saying, "Sacrifice yourselves for sinners, and say many times, especially whenever you make some sacrifice: *O Jesus, it is for love of You, for the conversion of sinners, and in reparation for the sins committed against the Immaculate Heart of Mary.*"[35] And Sr. Lucia recalled years later, "It must have been this sight [of Hell] which caused me to cry out, as people say they heard me. Terrified and as if to plead for succour, we looked up at Our Lady, who said to us, so kindly and so sadly: 'You have seen hell where the souls of poor sinners go. To save them, God wishes to establish in the world devotion to my Immaculate Heart. If what I say to you is done, many souls will be saved and there will be peace.'"[36]

[35] cf. Sr. Lucia, *Fatima in Lucia's Own Words*, 176.
[36] Ibid.

#35

I would like to return to that erroneous and yet widespread opinion that you, Antonia, recalled, namely that Hell is empty. What effects does this opinion have on living out faith?

IT'S SIMPLY DEVASTATING. ACCEPTING this idea means that at the end of life, everything will have the same outcome. Whether I love God and my neighbor or hate God and my neighbor, the result is always the reward of Heaven. Therefore, conversion, *metanoia*, changing one's mentality, would make no sense. The works of mercy would make no sense. And this goes against the teaching of the Gospel.

In order to teach about this in catechism, and thinking about those who believe that Hell does not exist or is empty, Carlo wrote down this extract from the *Diary* of St. Faustina Kowalska, the saint of Divine Mercy:

> Today, I was led by an Angel to the chasms of hell. It is a place of great torture; how awesomely large and extensive it is! The kinds of tortures I saw: the first torture that constitutes hell is the loss of God; the second is perpetual remorse of conscience; the third is that one's condition will never change; the fourth is the fire that will penetrate the soul without destroying it — a terrible suffering, since it is purely spiritual fire, lit by God's anger; the fifth torture is continual darkness and a terrible suffocating smell, and despite the darkness, the devils and the souls of the damned see each other and all the evil, both of others and their own; the sixth torture is the constant company of Satan; the seventh torture is horrible despair, hatred of God, vile words, curses and blasphemies.... I would have died at the very sight of these tortures if the omnipotence

of God had not supported me. Let the sinner know that he will be tortured throughout all eternity, in those senses which he made use of to sin. I am writing this at the command of God, so that no soul may find an excuse by saying there is no hell, or that nobody has ever been there, and so no one can say what it is like.

I, Sister Faustina, by the order of God, have visited the abysses of hell so that I might tell souls about it and testify to its existence. I cannot speak about it now; but I have received a command from God to leave it in writing. The devils were full of hatred for me, but they had to obey me at the command of God. What I have written is but a pale shadow of the things I saw. But I noticed one thing: that most of the souls there are those who disbelieved that there is a hell. When I came to, I could hardly recover from the fright. How terribly souls suffer there! Consequently, I pray even more fervently for the conversion of sinners. I incessantly plead God's Mercy upon them. O my Jesus, I would rather be in agony until the end of the world, amidst the greatest sufferings, than offend You by the least sin.[37]

The two stories that I recalled, that of Fatima and that of St. Faustina, refer to visions. The children of Fatima and St. Faustina learned through images. We, too, learn through sensorial experience, often from images seen with the eyes or produced and impressed through our imagination. And the two stories also speak of places. But notice how they said that the flames were spiritual, not physical. And finally, these are apparitions that seek to orient each one of us toward conversion of life and toward faith in God who is loving and saving Mercy.

[37]   Maria Faustina Kowalska, *Divine Mercy in My Soul* (Stockbridge: Marian Press, 2005), no. 741

#36

Besides the sports you mentioned, did Carlo have any hobbies?

HE HAD MANY HOBBIES. And as is normal for youth, they changed over the course of his maturation.

When he was a little child, video games like PlayStation, Game-Cube, XBox, and Game Boy started to circulate. He really liked them. On his own initiative, without our having to say anything to him, he set a time limit for his use of video games: one hour per week. Even at that age, he knew that they could become an addiction; he had read how in the United States, his peers were being sent to video-game detox centers, and in the worst cases they even suffered epileptic seizures.

As he got older, he received some gifts that transformed his free time: a photo camera and a digital video camera. He was quite talented at making short films with his friends and also with Rajesh, who in general played the role of the spy, or with his maternal grandmother, Luana, and with our dogs. They were action films that displayed a keen sense of irony as well. He put his photographic abilities to use in gathering a vast amount of material with which he conceived and produced exhibits on eucharistic miracles and the volume *Eucharistic Miracles and the Christian Roots of Europe*, together with Sergio Meloni, edited by Edizioni Studio Domenicano. It is a very important collection. Previously, nothing of its kind had been collected, combining photos and documents on all the eucharistic miracles; there were only essays or booklets dedicated to individual events or groups of events. It has reached its third edition and has been translated into other languages.

As a boy and even more so as an adolescent, his favorite hobby became information technology, with its many applications. Carlo always excelled in mathematics and in other scientific subjects. He developed a remarkable ability to produce programs with the most complex computer languages. Two university professors in computer engineering, friends of ours whom we visited with frequently in Milan, were positively amazed by his gifts. Carlo, as usual, made light of it: he wore a white t-shirt and a pair of fake glasses to make him look like an adult, and he stuck to the shirt a sign that said "computer scientist." When he was nine, he started to study university-level textbooks on computer science that we bought at Milan Polytechnic. Without having attended any courses, he was able to program in Java, C, C++, and Ubuntu, and elaborate in 3D with Adobe and Maya Suites.

Given that he was so capable and always ready to help, everyone started asking him to explain and help us in the use of the PC, including Rajesh, Grandma Luana, and also his classmates. This was another field in which he gave proof of his fraternal charity: dedicating time to others, growing in goodness with his talents, building something excellent, and transmitting to his neighbor his computer skills.

At the end of middle school, he helped many of his classmates by preparing PowerPoint drafts of their term papers for the examinations. With a young man studying computer engineering, he constructed the website of our parish, Santa Maria Segreta, in Milan. During his two years at Leone XIII High School, he continued to put his computer talents at the service of others, whether his classmates or the school itself. During the summer of 2006, he dedicated much of his free time to constructing a website that presented the apostolate and volunteer work managed by the Jesuits for the poor and needy.

To our great surprise, Pope Francis presented Carlo as a model in his use of the means of communication. He did so in the

Post-Synodal Apostolic Exhortation to Young People and to the Entire People of God, *Christus Vivit*:

> I remind you of the good news we received as a gift on the morning of the resurrection: that in all the dark or painful situations that we mentioned, there is a way out. For example, it is true that the digital world can expose you to the risk of self-absorption, isolation and empty pleasure. But don't forget that there are young people even there who show creativity and even genius. That was the case with the Venerable Carlo Acutis.
>
> Carlo was well aware that the whole apparatus of communications, advertising and social networking can be used to lull us, to make us addicted to consumerism and buying the latest thing on the market, obsessed with our free time, caught up in negativity. Yet he knew how to use the new communications technology to transmit the Gospel, to communicate values and beauty.
>
> Carlo didn't fall into the trap. He saw that many young people, wanting to be different, really end up being like everyone else, running after whatever the powerful set before them with the mechanisms of consumerism and distraction. In this way they do not bring forth the gifts the Lord has given them; they do not offer the world those unique personal talents that God has given to each of them. As a result, Carlo said, "everyone is born as an original, but many people end up dying as photocopies." Don't let that happen to you![38]

---

[38] Pope Francis, *Christus Vivit*, March 25, 2019, n. 104–106. https://www.vatican.va/content/francesco/en/apost_exhortations/documents/papa-francesco_esortazione-ap_20190325_christus-vivit.html.

#37

Every now and then, you have mentioned the fact that Carlo was a catechist. Can you tell us more about this?

THIS WAS FROM 2002–2003. Carlo was in his first year of middle school, and he came to us to ask if he could teach catechism with some of his friends who were just a little older than he was. Appointed by the parish priest, Msgr. Gianfranco Poma, they sought to prepare the children for Confirmation. We knew that his studies were taking up much of his time. We didn't want his schoolwork to suffer for it. And so we told him bluntly that he had our permission on condition that he continued to do well in school. He was faithful to this commitment for several years. He was always very satisfied and enthusiastic about the meetings that he organized energetically. The goal he set for himself with the catechism children was to propose that they become saints. And so he devised a kit for becoming a saint:

> "I want to share with you some of my special secrets that will help you to reach the goal of holiness in a hurry. Always remember that you, too, can become a saint! First of all, you must want to be one with all your heart, and if you still do not feel this desire, you have to ask for it insistently from the Lord.

> 1. Try to go to Mass every day and to receive Holy Communion.

> 2. If you can, take some moments to make eucharistic adoration before the tabernacle where Jesus is truly present, and you'll see how your level of holiness will rise!

3. Remember to recite the Holy Rosary every day.

4. Read a passage of Sacred Scripture every day.

5. If you can, go to Confession every week, even for your venial sins.

6. Make good resolutions to help others and do good deeds for the Lord and Our Lady.

7. Ask your Guardian Angel for help, for he must become your best friend."

#38

Those who knew Carlo (we have already heard from many of them) remember him as an enthusiastic boy, vivacious, obedient, and free. I ask Andrea: Is there not a contradiction in these qualities? Obedient, yet free and vivacious?

FREEDOM IS SITUATED AT the apex of man's desires; it can be said that it is a constituent part of the human person. For young people, freedom has a particular fascination because they have been subjected from birth to the authority of their parents and educators and are easily taken in by the possibility of liberating themselves from that authority. And so, it is so important to help them in discerning freedom's true nature. Generally, freedom is understood as the absence of exterior constraints in one's life, something that undoubtedly carries great importance, especially if it's a matter of being free of unjust constraints. Consider that politically, as children of the French Revolution, our society dedicates all its efforts to constructing democratic systems capable of keeping us free from tyranny, even though doing so leads us back into new forms of dictatorship.

Nevertheless, as they grow up, young people quickly discover that this liberty, understood as the absence of material constraints, continuously runs into obstacles that often appear insurmountable. First, because we find ourselves in time and space. Time runs ineluctably in one direction; we can live only in the present moment, and lost time can never be recovered. Given our current knowledge of physics, it seems that any object that has mass can move from one place to another only with a great expenditure of energy and cover distances that are laughable compared to the "infinite" distances in the universe. The vicissitudes of life, from birth to death, are subject to an infinite number of elements that do not depend on our will. We did not choose to come into this life nor where to be born, in which country in the world and in which family, nor the people we encounter, nor the circumstances we have to contend with, and so forth.

If young people are deceived with the hope of being able to free themselves from all these unavoidable constraints, we set them on the path of being failures from birth who seek nothing but the possibility of evading this world through distractions that are more or less licit. But how is it possible that the human soul has such a strong desire for something out of its grasp? Happiness depends on the certainty of being able to attain what we desire. Are we constitutionally condemned then to unhappiness? Or do we set our desires on things that will never satiate us?

Why do we tell our kids, "What's important is that you have fun," or "What's important is your health," or "You have to study because if you aren't successful in your career, you're a failure"? Healthy enjoyment, good health, and justly paid employment are all good things for which we must thank God if we have them. But it is by no means certain that we will have them, and they might not last if we do. In fact, we should say clearly that we know for certain that they won't last. Carlo made use of all the good things of this world, but the world was not his treasure. This is the problem: we are too much in the habit of seeking treasures where they are not to be found. And freedom from material constraints is one of these false treasures.

We are evidently beings endowed with freedom, a freedom we are continuously called to exercise through our choices. Even before being illuminated by faith, each one of us knows that there is a freedom that cannot be subject to constraints by anyone because it is immaterial: the freedom to desire or to love what we want. And so, even with our human faculties, we can intuit that the very essence of human life must be tied to this freedom and that, as a consequence, the use our young people make of it will determine the degree of success in their lives.

If we allow ourselves to be enlightened by our faith, everything will become clear, simple, and wonderful. God Himself, the Omnipotent, Love, the Greatest Good, knocks at the door of our heart and says to us: *I am Love; I created you to love and to be loved; do you desire this Love?* If we answer yes, we know with certainty that we will be heard because He has promised us this. This is the essence and the reason for our freedom. How could God offer us His love if He had not first given us a spiritual soul capable of freedom, of being able to say yes to Love in the same way in which we say yes to our beloved in the celebration of the sacrament of Matrimony? The freedom to love is tied to the faculties of our spiritual soul: the intellect and the will. The intellect proposes the good to us, and with the will we choose to love the good. We must have the humility to understand—not without the aid of grace—that God has arranged for us to be inserted into His divine life through the sacraments that He has instituted.

So, the task of parents is immensely simplified. The health of our children, their future career, all the good things of life are no longer the desired objective, but are downgraded to mere means for obtaining the Goal, which is God. We must teach our children that, contrary to the desires of this world—desires that are often realized but quite often lead to failure and therefore leave us suspended in a state of fear, so that we run to various distractions (this is the origin of the phrase "What's important is that you have fun")—contrary, as I was saying, to the desires of this world, a sincere and steadfast desire for God will absolutely not fail because the only requirement is to desire it resolutely and to act accordingly, saying yes to all the good things that the Lord proposes for us, with the help of the grace that He will never deny us if we do not oppose it. If the Good Thief was able to respond to grace, we and our children will be able to also. The problem is that this comes at a high price because we do not want to renounce our false treasures. We have to commit the time we have in this life in a continuous yes said with ever greater love, determination, and resolution, and a no to everything that opposes our obtaining treasure in Heaven. And the Lord will provide all the material and spiritual things we need during our journey.

Through the particular providence of the Lord, Carlo was able to benefit at a very young age from a special interior unity and harmony that was continually renewed by his choice to place God in first place, and consequently to put into practice the commandment of love. Perhaps this word "commandment" jars our ears trained in the false freedom of this world. Isn't love a passion that we must follow in order to be happy?

Sentiments and passions come and go, grow and diminish, often due to psychological factors tied to biochemical processes in our brain. Teaching our young people to pursue their loves, understood as "whatever I feel," would be the equivalent of teaching them to be

Pinocchio without freedom. Pinocchio thought that he was free when he followed his desires. Well, we need to teach our youth that above all, love is an act of the will that reaches beyond our sentiments. In fact, in the sacrament of Matrimony, we do not promise to love our spouse only until another impulse of attraction erupts in our psyche, but rather we promise to love until death do us part. The commandment to love God and our neighbor must be understood in this way.

Why do saints attract so many people? Because they exercise their freedom well and we perceive that they are moved by true Love, without the falsehood, division, and malice that are necessarily present, often unconsciously, in those who choose to adore treasures other than the Highest Good, in those who choose false freedoms.

#39

We often speak of a general paradigm in the educational process. Antonia, in your opinion and on the basis of your experience, what paradigm can you suggest?

WELL, I'LL BEGIN WITH my life experience. During my infancy, I met various kids, often the children of my parents' friends. After so many years, I can see that they have had very difficult lives. And I can identify the cause: an upbringing that was too free, that lacked stable reference points and a general framework of lofty objectives.

Looking at the lives of these people, I notice that all of them had in common very permissive parents: from the time they were about ten, they were allowed to do things that were normally reserved for older kids. Above all, the period from twelve to fourteen was devastating for them. I remember a girl I liked to play with, the daughter of a friend of my grandmother. We saw each other especially in the summer when I went to visit my grandmother in Anzio. We played a lot, especially with animals and stuffed animals. I was in for a shock in the summer of 1978. I had just turned twelve, and she was a year younger than me. We had not seen each other for a year when I met up with her at the sea the following year. I found her completely different. She dressed like an adult already, wore makeup and high heels. She hung out with older girls, daughters of friends of the family, all of them victims of an educational method that I would dare to call "devastating." This girl totally ignored me, as if she had never known me. She began to go out in the evening with older boys who led her down the path of alcohol, cigarettes, and marijuana.

The following year, my friend was pregnant, and this was her salvation. Most of the others, in one way or another, ruined their lives with drugs, hanging out with groups flaunting their extreme political views, and having disordinate emotional lives. Among these young people, only one friend from my childhood, who was particularly dear to me, managed to save herself thanks to a terrible automobile accident, from which she came away with physical disabilities that allowed her to escape the drug scene.

Many parents think that what's good for their children is to satisfy them always by allowing them maximum freedom. Unfortunately, however, this comes with many risks. Recent studies in neurobiology on brain development have shown that at the basis of typical adolescent behaviors there are precise neurological drivers. If, on the one hand, formal thought is developed during adolescence, allowing one to reason in an abstract, innovative, and creative manner at the same time one finds the intensification of emotions that youth often struggle to regulate, this cerebral immaturity does not allow the young person to live his or her emotions in a peaceful way but with greater risk of disturbances such as anxiety and stress. During adolescence, the push toward gratification also becomes strong, and consequently the push to discover new experiences, often entailing risky behaviors.

For adolescents, the other becomes a mirror in which to see one's own fears and perplexities, construct one's own identity, and learn to recognize one's emotions. Professor Giacomo Rizzolatti, renowned for his important scientific discoveries in mirroring neurons, highlights that neurons, in addition to playing a decisive role in learning by imitation, also have a significant impact on the phenomenon of empathy: "They seem to have a role also in social interactions, helping us to understand the aims and emotions of the other person. ... Mirror neurons constitute the basis for knowing in an instant what the other wants, what emotion they're feeling, and how they're living an experience."[39] The bonds created during adolescence play a very important role throughout life. If they are lived poorly, they can influence negatively one's decisions and behaviors, to the point of pushing young people to assume dangerous and reckless attitudes merely to win the approval of others.

Most adolescents, unless they have a strong Christian education, will typically make their decisions not based on what is right but based on what is most gratifying in the moment, and this can lead them to doing things that are very dangerous, like taking drugs, abusing alcohol, and creating disordinate relationships. Furthermore, young people are often attracted by risk; we see this

---

[39] This is a summary of Rizzolatti's thought by Giancarlo Dimaggio, following an interview with Rizzolatti concerning his latest book, *Specchi nel cervello. Come comprendiamo gli altri dall'interno [Mirrors in the Brain: How We Understand Others from the Inside]*, June 4, 2019, https://www.stateofmind.it/2019/06/neuroni-specchio-rizzolatti/.

clearly in the use of social media, where they compete in posting videos showing themselves doing dangerous stunts as a means of self-gratification. Young people are particularly emotive and so are more inclined to aggressivity and impulsiveness, with inhibitions that are not yet well developed. I have read studies that highlight how the prefrontal cortex allows us to elaborate judgments and to make decisions evaluating the cost-benefit relationship. But in adolescents this cerebral area is still in a construction phase, and so action prevails over reflection in their case. Adolescents have the sensation of dominating the world, and they enjoy taking risks; dangerous driving, dangerous friendships, and the use of intoxicating substances all appear extremely attractive behaviors. A drug taken out of curiosity, out of the desire to be acknowledged, out of impulsivity, or simply in search for powerful sensations, induces the adolescent's brain to release dopamine in notable quantities. The adolescent's brain is very fragile and vulnerable, and this predisposes it to develop dependency.

Sports can be a strong ally for parents because they help young people to activate a system of cerebral compensation, to develop the cognitive and executive functions, to reinforce the will and thus the virtues of fortitude and perseverance, and to get involved in constructive social relationships.

Above all, they need to be liberated from the weight of a vision of life without faith, centered on themselves. A new liberating framework of reason is needed, one that shifts the gaze from the finite to the infinite, from our ego to God. Without our Lord Jesus Christ, we live closed within the space of the material and psychological world. Motivators teach us about positive thinking, but how can we think positively if all our satisfactions are transitory, every consolation is momentary, and the certainty of our life's approaching end looms over us like a dark cloud, threatening total dissolution? No; thanks to

God, this is not our reality. We sensed this all along, but faith gives us the certainty of it—provided our faith is not based on sentimentality but on the concrete events of revelation.

Whatever activity we carry out needs a rational framework, fixed points that we can hold on to. Our rational framework in facing the vicissitudes of life, and in particular in raising children, cannot do without faith. We believe that God is our highest good, the greatest goodness, beauty, wisdom, truth, justice, omnipotence, mercy. We believe that He is Father, Son, and Holy Spirit, and we believe also the revealed truths that the Church has handed down. Thus, we know that life is a gift and that love is not an imposition but a proposal and that throughout life we undergo trials that allow us to give our yes to God and a steadfast no to everything that opposes Him. And in this way, we receive the gift of eternal beatitude in God.

We must first cultivate our faith. Do we believe that God wants what's best for us and that He is the one working in us to bring this about to the degree that we allow Him to do so? Or do we often prefer our vices to His love? The idea of being liberated from a vice terrorizes us, as if we had to amputate part of ourselves. Are we not convinced of the beauty of God, by chance? Of the wonder of the virtues that He desires personally to pour into us? Pagan philosophers praised the human virtues and the opportunity they offer to avoid becoming slaves of our passions. How is it that we who enjoy the privilege of faith do not perceive the sublimity of our call to become participants in divine life? Why do we not desire to free ourselves from all that distances us from our rightful treasure?

Once we convince ourselves of the beauty of our destination, we only have to employ the means of attaining it.

Parents receive a precious and difficult task. Just as they draw on material means for the good of their children, so, too, they are obliged to draw on the supernatural means that the Lord provides, directly in prayer and indirectly through the sacraments dispensed by the ministers of the Church.

We need to understand that just as civil law bestows prerogatives on parents with respect to their dependent children, so, too, on the spiritual level it is parents who have the responsibility to preserve their children's spiritual health. No one would ever dream of neglecting the physical health of their children so as not to interfere in their freedom of choice. In the same way, we do not have the right to deprive them of the necessary care of their souls through the transmission of Faith, the teaching of prayer, and the administration of Baptism and the other sacraments of Christian initiation. It is a duty that parents carry out on behalf of their children, similar to their duty to enroll them in school.

I recently met a desperate mother who asked for my help: her two daughters, twelve and fourteen years old, did not want to go to Sunday Mass. The mother told me that she asked the advice of a priest, who told her not to force them to go. I then suggested that she look into the baptismal promises and reflect on the fact that she and her husband committed themselves before God to raise these two children in the Christian Faith and that it is their duty to take them to Mass, even if the girls do not want to go, and to place greater trust in the divine omnipotence. We know that the sacrament of the Eucharist works *ex opere operato*: it always operates because it is Jesus Christ, true God, at work, acting independently of the dispositions of the celebrant and of the participants. Certainly, the ideal scenario would be that the celebrant and participants at Mass were well disposed, in other words, living in God's grace so as to obtain the best fruits of the sacrament. But even if they are not well disposed, for example if they were to have some attachment to sin, the grace of the sacrament works nevertheless in the person and transforms them and slowly erodes their bad dispositions. Therefore, who can know how the grace of God will work in those two girls? Furthermore, in this case it is the faith of the parents that supplies for the lack of faith of the daughters, who later, when they come of age, will be able to choose whether to continue participating in Mass or not.

Let us deepen our faith then, strengthening our desire for God, who is our destination. And in this way, with the help of the Lord and with the fruit of the sacrament of Matrimony, we will know how best to raise and educate our children. If things are not going well, let us not be discouraged but place everything in the Lord's hands. And let us not forget to tell our children no sometimes, loud and clear.

Adolescents are in search of role models and heroes to identify with. For decades now, the "star system" has dominated, proposing heroes and celebrities from movies, sports, and music, and in more recent years from social media. Without realizing it, young people enter a mechanism of identification and simultaneously of projection. Celebrities and their fans are a large factor, through their various roles, in the success of movies and songs or the spread of an athletic discipline. But wait a minute. Look at the lifestyles, the human traits, that our kids are imbibing. The behavioral models being conveyed or exalted by these celebrities often center on getting high, rebellion, and sex.

As parents and educators, we have the possibility and the responsibility of producing true celebrities: saints. The living tradition of the Church teaches us to look to the life of Jesus above all, and then to the lives of the saints, to learn the art of living.

We who claim to be believers, do we really believe that the life of Jesus and the lives of the saints are lives of true success? And if we believe this is the case, why do we not propose them?

#40

What is the importance of the sacrament of Matrimony in the process of raising children, do you think?

"WHAT THEREFORE GOD HAS joined together, let not man put asunder" (Matt. 19:6). This expression alludes to a revolutionary invention. God, creating man and woman, wanted to elevate marriage to the dignity of a sacrament, bringing it into the arena of the supernatural, to the point of touching eternal life. He united spouses at creation and makes them His personal collaborators. And this is the important point. By refusing this, we have opened the door to all the separations that undo the family, reducing the sacrament to a simple contract, to a mere human custom, transitory and subject to the winds of opinion and mood swings. But in our fluctuating society that has abandoned the constraints of social conventions, if we are not bound to a unifying and efficacious principle that is above man and comes from God, it is impossible to resist the centrifugal forces that are tearing families apart today more than ever before.

In the opinion of many, marriage has been emptied of its most profound meaning, that of being a sacrament, the work of Christ's love for the spouses, signifying and producing divine life, giving sanctifying grace in their lives in a direct, immediate, and most personal way. Husband and wife are ministers of this sacrament and are in direct, immediate, and personal contact with the Most Holy Trinity. This is the relationship that the Most Holy Trinity has desired. It is Jesus who explains to us the sacramentality of marriage. It is a sacrament because it is the relationship between man and woman on a supernatural plane, the relationship between man and woman by means of the grace that is administered. Marriage must be lived following this perspective, as the administration of the sacrament, where administration means the proper use of the sacrament; every time this use does not occur, one commits the sin of omission since the sacrament must be used, administered, according to God's intentions. And the intentions of God are the sanctity of husband and wife, their growth in reciprocal love, and the procreation of children. Like the sacrament of Holy Orders, the sacrament of Matrimony is a social sacrament, namely in light of the communion between husband and wife; it is to their advantage and the advantage of the Church and of the generation of children. Through procreation, we collaborate with the permanence, the continuity, and the richness of the human race. Thus, husband and wife must not abstain from the use of marriage because otherwise they would fail in their sacramental duty to procreate as the Lord wills for the good of the human race.

Here, the human race itself is at stake, creation itself is at stake. We must enter this mentality and remember that man and woman married in the Church have in their hands a patrimony of grace to administer, to increase, to enrich, making it circulate in the family; they have in their hands the good of human generation.

"What therefore God has joined together, let not man put asunder." Grace for the good of humanity is at stake here. Becoming incarnate, Jesus could have sought any other system to assume human nature. He assumed it, however, in the most common form: the family. He inserted Himself into the reality of the family. He wanted to become an integral part of a human family. Keep in mind that, when God, in the Trinity of Persons, created rational being, He created it male and female, so that the two could help each other to live in God's love. This communion of life and love is consecrated and blessed by God Himself. In the fullness of time, Jesus elevated marriage to the dignity of a sacrament, a sign and action that produces sanctifying grace. Grace is, then, the fabric, the substance, the essence, the reason, the motive for the family entity. It is the cement that unites it. It is the reason for its being. If there is no grace, there is no family. For this reason, the family constituted by the sacrament of Matrimony must remain in a state of grace. In God's plan and in the words of Jesus, grace represents the essence of marriage.

Marriage, according to the Christian Faith, is founded on the grace of God and is a source of grace over the course of life. Thus, grace must be the constant fabric of living out one's marriage. The sacrament of Matrimony does not allow mortal sin to enter the home of Christian spouses. Being a sacrament, marriage renders the home a micro-church. Thus, we can affirm that every mortal sin in the family is a sacrilege. Members of the family, at the moment they feel they are not in God's grace, must immediately say, "Lord, I repent," and determine to confess their sin as soon as possible, as their circumstances permit. Then grace can constitute once more the interior of the Christian family. The Holy Family of Nazareth is holy because grace reigns there. Imitating the Holy Family means resolving to live constantly in sanctifying grace.

Sr. Lucia of Fatima prophesied, "A time will come when the decisive battle between the kingdom of Christ and Satan will be over marriage and the family."[40] The Holy Family of Nazareth gives us the same Jesus who gives Himself in a special way in the consecrated bread and wine. It guides men to receive Him in their families, to allow Him to be born in their hearts. The Virgin Mary "wrapped him in swaddling cloths" (Luke 2:7) as soon as He was born. Her maternity immediately expressed itself in caring for Him, protecting Him from the cold. That gesture encourages us, too, to care for the Child-God and for our children as well.

[40] Letter of Sr. Lucia of Fatima to Cardinal Carlo Caffarra, cited in https://aleteia.org/2017/05/19/exclusive-cardinal-caffarra-what-sr-lucia-wrote-to-me-is-being-fulfilled-today.

We have already spoken about our pilgrimage to Barcelona. I recall it here in reference to the Holy Family. Carlo was enraptured at seeing the Basilica of the Sagrada Família designed by Antoni Gaudí. He was enthralled not only by its architectural beauty but also by the idea it transmitted: in a moment of such great crisis for the institution of the family, the work of Gaudí is the divine response to so much devastation. Whereas society no longer comprehends the value of the family and so destroys it, Gaudí reconstructs it metaphorically through his Sagrada Família. Gaudí was convinced that man's originality consists in returning always to the origins, namely to God, to creation, of which man and woman have always been protagonists. The family of Nazareth is the perfect example of cooperation in creation and redemption, in complete abandonment to the divine will.

#41

Is there an educational model that inspires you in particular?

EVERY EDUCATIONAL MODEL OUGHT to permit each person to realize that supernatural destiny to which we are called, the final end to which every activity of our lives must tend. *Respice finem*, i.e., keep your eyes on the end. The supernatural means are first of all the sacraments, prayer, the Word of God, and in particular the Holy Mass and eucharistic adoration! The aim of the Catholic ascetical tradition is to help souls resemble God more and more. In all the things we do, it is imperative to consider the end we are proposing to attain. To us, educating a young person in a Christian way means helping him to "conform" himself increasingly to Christ.

We live in a fallen and repaired state of nature, *in statu naturae lapsae et per Christum reparatae.* "Conformity" to Christ, given Original Sin, implies an effort to change, to reform. Original Sin has deformed the image of Christ in us. Thanks to Baptism, divine life—sanctifying grace—has been given to us, making us adopted children of God in the image of Christ who is the only begotten Son. Weakness, fragility, and woundedness remain in us, however, which only a virtuous life can heal and eliminate. The education parents give must help to carry out that reform of the child "deformed" by the old Adam and the old Eve, to "conform" the child to the New Adam who is Christ and the New Eve who is the Blessed Virgin Mary.

The sooner we undertake this life of reform and fortification, the better. If the sapling grows crooked, Don Bosco said, it will be quite difficult to straighten the mature tree later. What is important is that we help our children to "conform" themselves to Christ, both interiorly and exteriorly, and to establish a friendship with Him, trusting Him completely. God has destined us to be the image and likeness of His Son. Given that our destiny is supernatural, the way the Lord wants us to raise our children will make use of supernatural means. It will make use, first of all, of sanctifying grace received mainly through the sacraments. Without the grace of Christ, all our efforts and natural means will remain ineffective. Jesus Himself said, "Abide in me, and I in you. As the branch cannot bear fruit by itself, unless it abides in the vine, neither can you, unless you abide in me. I am the vine, you are the branches. He who abides in me, and I in him, he it is that bears much fruit, for apart from me you can do nothing" (John 15:4–5).

The pedagogical method followed by Don Luigi Orione, the great student and disciple of St. John Bosco, can help us in this matter. Don Orione called it the "Christian-paternal method." In every man, he saw and served Christ. Before assisting the person needing care, he sought to contemplate in that person the image of God, to the point that love for the person (a son of God) and worship of God the Father no longer had such clear and distinct boundaries but reciprocally implied and reinforced each other.

For Don Orione, it was necessary to develop in each person that "divine presence" and to make this the motivating reason and aim of every parent and educator.

Michelangelo could contemplate in the mass of marble the inchoate work he wanted to produce. His action as a sculptor consisted in "drawing out" the figure he wanted to have emerge. Every act of educating needs to contemplate the Highest Good, which must be the sole inspiration. Don Orione experienced and developed his own Christian-paternal pedagogical method, re-elaborating the preventive method of Don Bosco that he encountered as a youth frequenting the Salesians.

One of the fundamental instructions of the Christian-paternal method consists in "taking care." He always recommended, "Love them in the Lord like your own brothers, take care of their health, of their education, and of all their good: may they feel your interest in raising them ... For you, there should be no ungrateful or sterile terrain that, through long patience, cannot finally be made to bear fruit; the same is true of man." Don Orione's models were the family of Nazareth and all the families inspired by its human, spiritual, and practical attitudes.

#42

At the end of this interview, can you offer some suggestions for raising our children in a Christian manner?

GLADLY. WE'LL DRAW FROM our experience just a brief summary, not exhaustive of course, but propositional.

As parents, let us make every effort to adopt behaviors that are coherent with our Faith: let us offer the example of our behavior before offering our words. The true adhesion of our children to the Faith comes about through attraction, not by forcing the matter. If we do not wish to be saints, if we are attached to our compromises, on what authority can we ask our children to live coherently? Being a Christian means that our neighbor must see in us a reflection of Jesus.

If we make a mistake, we must admit our error. We should not be afraid of asking for forgiveness. We are all walking along the path, parents and children, and we all have our fragilities. What's important is that we are not attached to our defects and vices but that we desire to grow in virtue.

Let us allow our children to have the experience of being understood and loved, regardless of the errors they might commit. Our children will then feel included in the circuit of conjugal love.

Parents, whether united or not, should not speak ill of their spouse and should excuse any eventual failings.

Let us pray every day with our children. The family that prays together stays together. Let us train ourselves in prayer to desire what we say with our words; much of prayer is training our desire to be finalized always in God. Let us invite our children to personal prayer as well, from the moment we rise in the morning. A suitable moment for prayer together can be before going to bed, dedicating time for an examination of conscience and for thanksgiving to God for all that He has given throughout the day, and to prayers for special intentions. Let us find a way to pray the Rosary daily, together if possible. There are so many graces that Our Lady has promised for those who recite it with devotion. If they are accustomed from a young age, children will recite it gladly; trips in the car can also be good moments to recite the Rosary. Finally, the Liturgy of the Hours prayed together can be a moment of great grace.

Let us read the Word of God together with our children; we cannot face the challenges of life without a compass. The Word scrutinizes us, guides us, challenges us, heals us, liberates us from the slavery of the world, and helps us to see things from the divine viewpoint.

Let us go to Mass together on Sunday, on the other days of obligation, and, if possible, even on weekdays; let us trust in the healing and liberating power of God who works through the sacraments. Even if at times our children go to church against their will, their parents' faith compensates for their lack of faith. All our educational strategies are useless without the grace of God; we must be steadfast in the obligation of the Sunday Mass, with sweet firmness. If possible, let us pause for some time before the Blessed Sacrament in adoration.

Let us all go to Confession weekly, or if that's not possible, at least monthly, remembering to mention our minor failings, which are nevertheless great spiritual impediments to attaining virtue; great are the graces that we receive in a well-made Confession.

If possible, let us have at least one or two meals together each day, without the TV or cell phones; these are opportune times for being together. Let us accompany meals with a prayer of thanksgiving; all good things we receive, even if they are the fruit of our own work, we must see them as coming directly from God.

Let us reprimand our children, avoiding bitterness; let us compensate as soon as possible for any eventual harshness with little gestures of affection, like a sincere kiss. Let us apply Don Bosco's preventive method. His words tell us,

> Through the ages there have been two systems used in the education of the young: preventive and repressive. The repressive approach consists in making the law known to the students and then supervising them in order to detect transgressions, inflicting, wherever necessary, the merited punishment.... Quite otherwise, I would say its very opposite, is the preventive system. It consists in making known the rules and regulations of an Institute, and then supervising in such a way that the students are always under the vigilant eye of the Director and the assistants, who like loving fathers will converse with them, act as guides in every event, counsel them and lovingly correct them, which is as much as to say, will put the students into a situation where they cannot do wrong. This system is all based on reason, religion and loving-kindness.[41]

Make known to your children the rules that must be respected and always maintain an adult presence. Exceptions must be exceptions. Tantrums are not the moment for making an exception.

Let us strengthen the message of the Word of God by reading and listening to catechesis, stories of the saints and of Marian apparitions recognized by the Church, and recognized miracles, especially

---

41 John Bosco, "The Preventive System in The Education of the Young," critical edition, ed. P. Braido, trans. P. Laws, https://www.sdb.org/en/Don_Bosco/Writings/Writings/The_preventive_system_in_the_education_of_the_young__Critica.

Eucharistic miracles. Let us dedicate time to consolidating the faith of the family, welcoming with joy the signs the Lord wants to give us. Let us accustom our children to loving the perfume of Paradise.

When the occasion arises in conversation, let us remind them of the order of priorities: what is important and what is less important. What counts is the beauty of the soul, not exterior appearances. Success in life is measured only by the level of charity we have attained.

Let us eliminate phrases like "What's important is having fun," or "What's important is your health," or any discourse that infers that what counts is being successful in life (from the world's point of view), anything that would imply that whoever has not attained it is a failure. Instead, let us teach the beauty of committing ourselves to doing well the things done for love of God. The mentality of the world is presented as an implacable judge that measures physical performance, intelligence, wealth, or success in any material activity. It is said that where there's a will, there's a way; but much also depends on the circumstances, and for this reason many people actually find themselves before insurmountable obstacles that impede them from realizing their material desires. Instead, our Creator commands us to love and to measure the success of our lives based on the charity that we have attained. He imposes on us something that is within the reach of every man, for the simple reason that sanctification is not a process of addition but one of subtraction (Carlo loved to say this): less of me, to leave space for God. A life of success will be a life in which we succeed in placing God always in first place. Realizing this objective will require much effort on our part in combating the vices that keep us from growing in virtue.

During our travels, let us add a stage to visit sanctuaries, especially those in which the Virgin Mary has left a sign of purification, like the miraculous waters of Lourdes, in Caravaggio, or Collevalenza; they will be moments of grace and conversion for the entire family, reminding us of the importance of our Baptism. If we visit a church, let us pause before the tabernacle where Jesus' presence in the Eucharist is indicated by the red lamp, to thank God and to adore Him.

Let us train our children in charity, encouraging them to make little gestures of complete gratuitousness, in the family and outside of it.

Let us train them in temperance, giving them an example by moderation in eating and by offering little sacrifices. Let us teach them the difference between sentiment (what I am feeling) and will (what I want or desire). Feeling is different from wanting. We must realize what we want, as distinguished from what we feel, and we must avoid putting ourselves in the condition of longing for something we cannot have.

Let us purify our language, eliminating indecent words and coarse conversation; let us reprimand our children on this matter before it becomes a habit for them; a time for decent speech and a time for letting ourselves go is not acceptable. Christians are not called to be people divided within themselves but to be united around one vivifying and liberating principle: the Love of God.

Let us preserve their purity, protecting them from all the impure images that inundate our lives. Let us start by limiting the television and lead by example; if we do not want to be stung by a scorpion, we have to stay away from it. Special attention must be given to avoiding exposure to pornography, a downright spiritual poison.

Let us invite young people to preserve their sense of modesty. Nice clothing must first of all clothe us; a person's beauty is in the soul and must transpire from the face, not in the form of the body. Modern Western society affirms that it is founded on freedom. Good, then we are free not to follow fashions that do not please God. In the apparitions of Fatima, Our Lady warned that fashions were coming that would gravely offend our Lord.

Let us remind them of the great dignity of the human being, created in God's image.

Let us place limits on certain activities: television, video games, cell phones, etc. Carlo limited himself to an hour of video games per week. Let us instead encourage reading upright books or doing manual activities, or maybe helping out with housework, or playing healthy sports.

Let us teach them to thank God and neighbor and not to complain; the difficulties of life must be presented to God without resentment; let us teach them to carry their cross in imitation of our Lord and offer it to God who will make it bear fruit for the sanctification of the world.

Let us teach them not to criticize their neighbor, since we cannot be sure we are any better; pride is the root of all evils.

Whatever arguments we might have must be concluded with reciprocal forgiveness; let us remind our children of the commitment to forgiving that we make every time we recite the Our Father. Lack of forgiveness is a cancer that kills the soul through suffocation, through a lack of love.

Let us take the necessary time to do well our task as parents. When we don't have time to do all this, perhaps we have not placed God in first place. Let us train ourselves in making renunciations and free ourselves from every attachment we might prefer to God. God desires our good and acts with sweetness in freedom. Let us not take our gaze from Him and from His inspirations, and all will go well. If we fall, or find ourselves in trouble, let us turn to Him with trust. Let us train ourselves in recognizing how much God has given us and ask Him for all we need. The happy person is the one who knows he can obtain all he desires: let us train ourselves then in desiring God and He will fill us with all good. That is His promise.

About the Authors

Antonia Salzano, born in Rome in 1966, and Andrea Acutis, born in Turin in 1964, are the parents of St. Carlo Acutis.

Giorgio Maria Carbone was born in Naples in 1969 and is a Dominican friar and priest. He is also the author of *Originals or Photocopies?* (Edizioni Studio Domenicano, Bologna 2021), in which he collects and comments upon all the phrases of Carlo Acutis that have been attributed to him by witnesses at the canonical process of the Archdiocese of Milan for his beatification.

Sophia Institute